2020
THE CHINA MENACE

Michael Farlander

Adam Wiseman

ISBN: 9781692649456
Independently published

CONTENTS

1

INTRODUCTION

China's hidden agenda has finally been revealed. After decades of feigning a pacifist rise by following former paramount leader Deng Xiaoping's strategy of "Hide our strength, bide our time," decades during which it built up by hook or by crook a powerful economy and military, China has finally shown its true colors, that of being a rising militaristic power that follows Mao Zedong's philosophy of "Political power grows out of the barrel of a gun." None other than Taiwan, which knows China better than any other country, succinctly described China's rise for what it truly is when in 2019 Taiwan's government said that China's claim of its "peaceful development" was the **"lie of the century."**

China is on course to becoming the most powerful country in the world, a status it held centuries ago during its heyday when the Middle Kingdom was a world power. Spearheaded by its supreme leader Xi Jinping and the Communist Party of China (CPC), China is working feverishly to realize the "China Dream," the dream of "Making China Great Again." Unfortunately, while such a grandiose effort to achieve greatness cannot but be lauded, the goal of China is more than just to become a strong and prosperous country. The goal of the Chinese leaders, and most Chinese for that matter, is to reshape the world order with a domineering China on top, and equally important to seek redress and exact revenge for the century of humiliation that China went through at the hands of Western and other powers.

The Chinese are not ones to forget their history or the past injustices that were inflicted on them, no matter how long ago. The Chinese are not the pacifist people that they feigned to be when China was weak and only embarking on its modernization drive. The Chinese know how to bide their time until the time is right, as their former leader Deng Xiaoping used to say. And the time is right! The Chinese are looking for a big payback against the countries that presumably wronged them one way or another, and that includes Western countries and most of China's neighbors, especially Russia and Japan. This strategy of communist China is clearly illustrated in the following figure, which shows how that country's foreign policy has evolved.

After the People's Republic of China was founded in 1949 under the leadership of the CPC, the country faced existential problems and had to focus on its domestic affairs. However, after a couple of decades of turmoil and power consolidation, the country started opening up to the outside world. And in a relatively short time span of three decades thereafter, China went from being a weak country focused on its internal affairs, to being an assertive and increasingly belligerent power on the world stage. In just half a century since its foundation, communist China has radically transformed itself and is now pursuing a strategy of world dominance.

In order to achieve its goal of world dominance, China

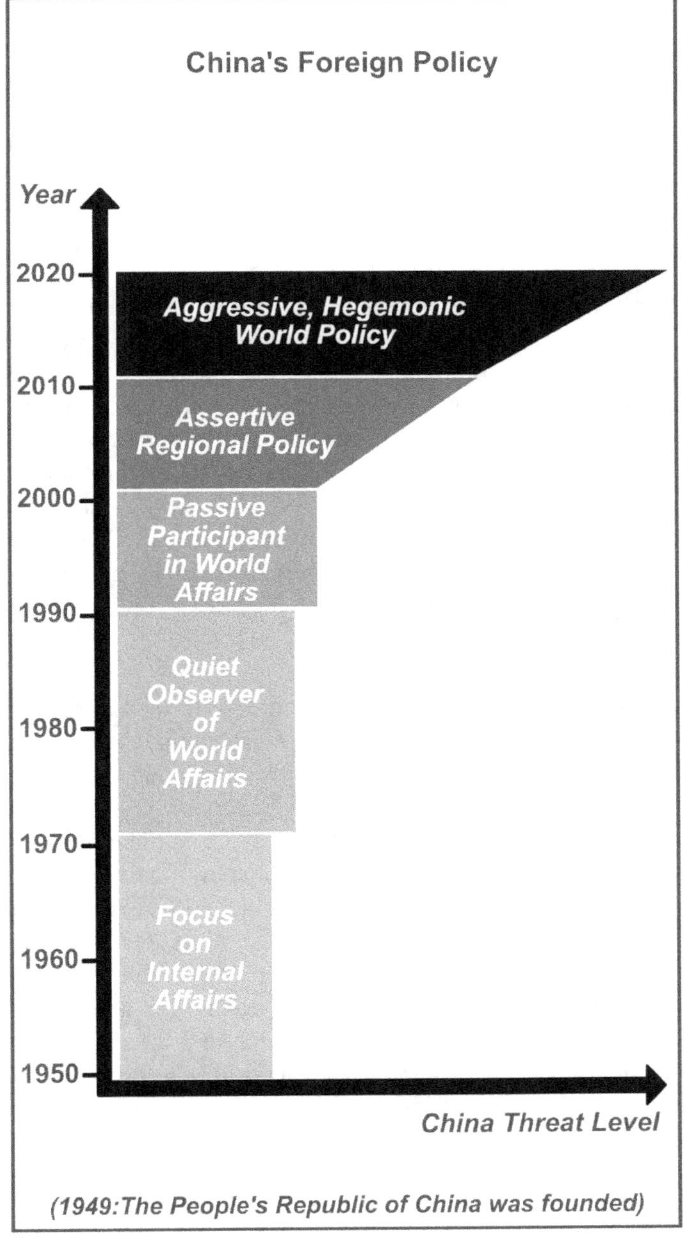
China's Foreign Policy
Year
2020
2010
2000
1990
1980
1970
1960
1950
Aggressive, Hegemonic World Policy
Assertive Regional Policy
Passive Participant in World Affairs
Quiet Observer of World Affairs
Focus on Internal Affairs
China Threat Level
(1949: The People's Republic of China was founded)

has been using a four-pronged strategy of relying on its economy, ideology, politics, and the military. In the economy, China has risen to become the world's biggest economy by some estimates, and is already using its economic might as a leverage or weapon, such as to gain concessions from trading partners, to bully unfriendly countries, and to gain influence around the world. In ideology, the CPC has basically succeeded in radicalizing the Chinese populace and envenoming it with not only extremely dangerous jingoism, but also with a deep-seated mistrust and even bitter hatred toward the West and other countries. In politics, China has shown its true Machiavellian colors by challenging and undermining anything Western, by promoting its totalitarian ideals around the world, and by pursuing a more and more belligerent and even hegemonic foreign policy. And in the military, China has built up formidable armed forces and has been flexing its military muscle through a defense budget that dwarfs those of its neighbors Russia, Japan and India.

China has been honing its strategy of becoming the dominant world superpower by weakening, neutralizing and eventually marginalizing the present superpower, the US. The facts are undeniable. In the economy, China has destroyed US manufacturing by maintaining an undervalued currency for ages. China has weakened or chased out US companies doing business in China through IP theft and a slew of protectionist measures, such as forcing them to share their technology with Chinese companies. China has also bought many US assets and controls a very significant chunk of America's debt. In ideology, China has been using soft power to swamp and sway the American mindset via its Confucius schools and other propaganda tools, such as international TV channels and radio stations. In politics, China has been succeeding in weaning countries from under Western influence,

China's Four-Pronged Strategy for Supremacy

- ❖ *Large-scale theft of Western IP*
- ❖ *Milking and weakening foreign companies*
- ❖ *Illegal subsidies and support of local companies*
- ❖ *Misuse of WTO*
- ❖ *Establishing own international bodies*

2 Ideology

- ❖ *Indoctrination of its masses*
- ❖ *Suppression of dissent*
- ❖ *Consolidation of power in CPC supreme leader*
- ❖ *International propaganda*

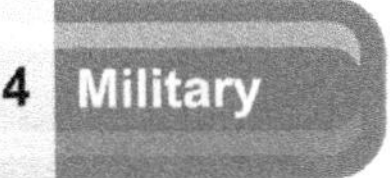

- ❖ *War on democracy*
- ❖ *Support of dictatorships*
- ❖ *Belligerent foreign policy*
- ❖ *Creating zones of influence around the world*

4 Military

- ❖ *Strong military*
- ❖ *Overseas bases*
- ❖ *Bullying and subjugation of neighbors*
- ❖ *Preparation for inevitable war with the US*

promoting its mode of governance around the world, and weakening any US resolve by using lobbying groups staffed by venal moneygrubbing American politicians and lawyers. And in the military, China has mounted a virtual all-out assault to contain and then overtake the US. Thus, China has developed the capability to incapacitate the US command-and-control structure, such as by testing satellite-killer missiles. It has been building the tools to limit the US ability to project power by deploying aircraft-carrier-killer missiles while building its own aircraft carriers and strong navy. It has built a string of naval bases that stretch from China to the South China Sea, the Indian Ocean, and all the way to Africa. It has built, tested, and started deploying stealth aircraft. It's suspected of planting bugs and backdoors in the products that its IT manufacturers export. It has manufactured fake and subpar components that go in US military systems. And it's been actively engaged in large-scale cyber-espionage to acquire sensitive US high tech.

China's world ambitions have become quite clear and the Chinese aren't afraid or shy anymore about expressing them. Once, at a meeting with US officials, a Chinese general suggested that China and the US divide up the Pacific Ocean between them, with Hawaii being the midpoint. The remark may have been said lightly, but it belies real Chinese beliefs and intentions. China now routinely and assertively asks the US to butt out of conflicts such as the ones regarding the South China Sea, the East China Sea, Taiwan, the Senkaku Islands, Tibet, Xinjiang, the Indian border, and so on. China now has or is building its own zones of influence around the world, such as in Southeast Asia, South Asia, Central Asia, Africa, Latin America, and even Europe.

China has become very confident in asserting itself on the world stage. Its policy now is: China is always right, deal with it! This is nothing more than a re-coinage of the old adage of *might is right*. China now wants to solve every conflict on its own terms. This doesn't sound like the policy of a pacifist country but rather the policy of a belligerent power. And things will only get worse as China keeps growing stronger. When China becomes the dominant global power, a "Pax Sinica" with a domineering China will rule the world.

For the naïve skeptics who believe the nonsense of China's peaceful rise, they need only look at what China has been doing politically, militarily, economically, socially, and even environmentally around the world. Politically, China lied about its rise and global intentions, has aggressively asserted itself on the world stage, is supporting dictatorships around the world, and is also winning the ideological war against Western democracy. Militarily, China has been aggressively building up its military might, bullying its neighbors, and projecting its military power on a global scale. Economically, China has used every unethical way to build up its economy at the expense of the West, and has been using its economic might to build a new economic world order to its liking. Socially, China exports corruption, crime and bad behavior around the world, and has trained its people to be jingoists and to mistrust and even hate foreigners like Westerners and the Japanese. Incredible as it may be in this day and age, China has even imprisoned millions of its non-Han people in concentration camps. And environmentally, China has been irresponsibly poisoning the whole planet's atmosphere on an unprecedented scale in the history of humankind and with total disregard for other countries' concerns, depleting the world's raw materials at alarming rates, and decimating wildlife all over the world. All of this is clear evidence of a domineering China with an agenda of dominating the world. China cannot be trusted when it talks about pacifism and international collaboration.

The problem with the American, and in general Western, approach to China is that Western leaders and intellectuals have always considered the Chinese as been similar to them in their human qualities and aspirations. The fact is that the Chinese are starkly different from Westerners, not just in their appearance but more importantly in their character. The West's naïve belief that the Chinese could be Westernized and made to live by the same standards is not only totally wrong but also very dangerous as it keeps on waiting for the Chinese to change while in fact the Chinese are changing the West.

Western government, academia and business leaders' naive and misguided approach to China has been grounded in the notion that as China developed and prospered, China would become a responsible power, and embrace the Western ideals of democracy and human rights. However, as has been demonstrated time and again over decades, China plays by its own rules. China believes in a win-win strategy where it wins the lion's share and the rest of the world "wins" the crumbs.

US presidents from Nixon to Obama, and even Trump, have all erroneously, naively, and foolishly believed that a richer China was better than a poor China. A poor China would have been easier to dominate and even partition. Obama, the quintessential shuck-and-jiving weakling, once proudly boasted, "I've been very explicit in saying that we have more to fear from a weakened, threatened China than a successful, rising China." What baloney! China not only treated him with total disdain and flagrant disrespect, but has proven him completely wrong.

The famous American saying of "Fool me once, shame on you. Fool me twice, shame on me" applies so aptly to US leaders. US administrations, from the time of Nixon to

Obama, should be utterly ashamed of themselves for having being played like fools by China for decades. Trump has shown signs of standing up for America and confronting China, but only time will tell whether he can maintain such an attitude and really defend America against China because even he has fallen to Chinese manipulation such as when he made a major policy reversal with regards to the Chinese company ZTE, going from branding it a national threat to immediately coming to its rescue.

The uncomfortable truth is that China has all along been engaged in a zero-sum game with the West, a game that it's winning. China is gradually but surely succeeding in becoming the most powerful country in the world. And this frightening scenario is not only the result of China's efforts but equally the result of the West's naïve, moronic, and cowardly accommodation.

It's truly a pity that the Chinese have been allowed to reach such a status. None other than the greatest human mind of all time, Einstein himself, said, "It would be a pity if these Chinese supplant all other races. For the likes of us the mere thought is unspeakably dreary." Einstein figured out the Chinese for what they truly were, that of being almost inhuman. He described them as "industrious, filthy, obtuse, herd-like people that were more like automatons than people."

Just as Einstein's Theory of Relativity has stood the test of time, his observations on the Chinese are just as lasting. Are the Chinese industrious? Yes, the Chinese work tirelessly and endlessly like machines. Are they filthy? Well, the Chinese are not exactly known for their hygiene, like the Japanese for example are. Are they obtuse? Yes, they are, especially to the West's ideals of democracy and human rights. Are they herd-like? Yes, they epitomize the herd mentality for wherever you see a Chinese, a great many follow. Are they more automatons than people? Observing them for a long time, one can't but admit that yes they are. They seem almost inhuman in their character and behavior. And most importantly, since Einstein didn't interact with the Chinese for any length of time, he didn't have the chance to discover their other great deficiencies: utter cruelty and innate deception. These Chinese traits of survival of the fittest and dog eat dog are probably the evolutionary factors that contributed to the Han being the largest racial group in the world.

Are some Chinese "OK"? Yes, but the problem is in their number. Maybe there are a million, or ten million, or even a hundred million OK-Chinese, but that still leaves out more than a billion problem-Chinese.

The "China Dream" is shaping up to be the West's nightmare.

2

ECONOMY

Rape by China. Death by China. These are the words of none other than US President Trump and the president of the National Trade Council on how China has caused great harm to the US economy and wrecked entire industries. How China succeeded in causing such great damage to the US economy is all part of China's strategy to overtake the West and gain world preeminence.

From early on in the founding of the People's Republic of China, its leaders knew full well that an essential step toward becoming a global superpower was to have a strong developed economy. They also knew that the West was very accommodating when it came to doing business, versus other spheres such as politics and military affairs. Thus, China embarked on an ambitious and unprecedented program of economic development through successive five-year plans. The guiding principle was to develop the economy as fast as possible, and at any cost. That meant orchestrating the biggest heist of Western riches that the world has ever known, and polluting our planet on an unprecedented scale. And China has succeeded in building a strong economy that according to some measurements is already the biggest in the world. And as expected, China is now using its economic superpower status to further its interests all around the world, to bully and punish countries that it deems unfriendly, to build a new economic world order, and to fund and deploy a global military power.

The biggest heist in world history

China is a country built on deceit. Indeed, from the time of Chairman Mao to the present, the country has been ruled by the Communist Party of China (CPC), a party that controls the country in a totalitarian and non-transparent way and through a system of institutionalized lies. There are many examples to illustrate this corrupt environment of deceit. For example, China claims that it's a democracy because in addition to the ruling communist party, there are a few other totally insignificant and subservient parties that are allowed to exist. Another example is that China still officially considers itself a communist country, or to use its cute nomenclature a "socialist country with Chinese characteristics," when the fact is that the gap between the rich and poor has reached alarming levels worse than in many capitalist countries. And another example is that China considers itself a market economy when the fact is that the government owns and controls almost everything, including the big enterprises, the banks, the stock exchanges, and so on.

This environment of deceit has pervasively permeated the modern Chinese psyche. The Chinese people have come to understand from watching their hypocritical leaders, who preach one thing and do the opposite, that such a corrupt mentality is the norm and the way to success. In particular, when it comes to doing business whether domestically or abroad, the Chinese can be shamelessly cunning and corrupt. According to WorldAudit.org and Transparency International, China is more corrupt than even some African and Middle Eastern countries.

Thus, from the time that China opened up to the rest of the world and started engaging in trade, it has done so with almost total disregard for business ethics. And the incredible thing is that this Chinese behavior of cunning and deceit was met in the West with wide-open arms because all the West could think about was the huge potential that the Chinese market represented.

And so the West and other countries engaged in trade with China in the hope that China would mend its corrupt and unethical business practices, and with the expectation of access to the Chinese market. The naïve approach of the West has always been that trade with China is a win-win strategy. However, China's perspective has always been that dealings with the West, whether in business or other spheres, are part of a zero-sum game that it must win. And years and decades passed, and the Chinese totally outplayed the West, not only through huge trade imbalances but also through the biggest heist of riches that the world has ever known.

According to multiple US Government sources, each year China steals more than $300 billion in intellectual property from the US, and that's only via cyber-hacking. Adding non-cyber theft would double that figure to $600 billion a year, according to the Commission on the Theft of American Intellectual Property, an independent US body including representatives from the public and private sectors. The losses to the US are astronomical. According to the National Cyber Strategy of the United States of America report released by the White House in September 2018, China engaged in cyber-enabled economic espionage

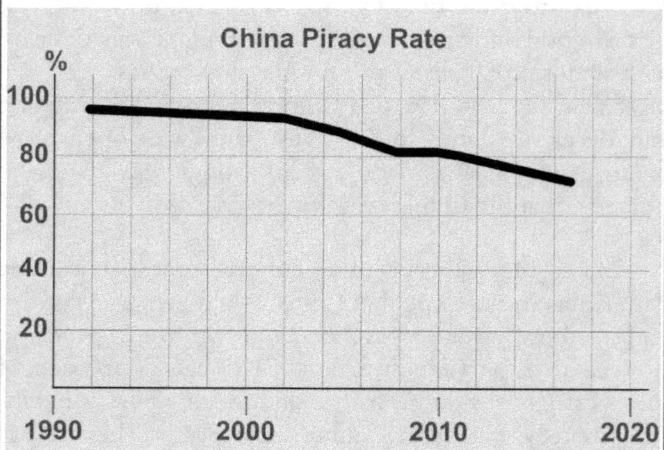

China Raping the US
China Piracy Rate
%
100
80
60
40
20
1990
2000
2010
2020
In 2015 alone,
China's hacking of
US intellectual property
cost the US economy losses
worth a whopping
$360 billion
And,
that figure becomes even much higher
when non-cyber losses are added.
Source: BSA, Counterintelligence and Security Center

and trillions of dollars of intellectual property theft. In 2018, Senator Rubio of Florida said about the Chinese, "They are basically conducting an all-out assault to steal what we've already developed and use it as the baseline for their development so they can supplant us as the leader in the most important technologies of the 21st century."

China has been conducting its unprecedented large-scale theft of US, and Western too, intellectual property by targeting companies, universities, research centers, organizations, government offices, and other entities and places by using a variety of ways including its intelligence services, non-traditional information-collecting agents, joint ventures, mergers and acquisitions, front companies, academic collaboration, research partnerships, and administrative reviews.

China's intelligence services conducted by its Ministry of State Security, an entity equivalent to the CIA and FBI combined, uses Chinese nationals and Chinese Americans in its missions. For instance, in 2015, a Chinese American pleaded guilty to the charge of conspiring to help China garner special nuclear technological know-how in violation of US laws. In 2017, a Chinese-American nuclear engineer was convicted of the same charge. In 2018, a General Electric engineer, a Chinese American, was arrested for stealing almost 20,000 files related to proprietary power-turbine technology. And in late 2018, Chinese agents were indicted for conducting unprecedented large-scale multi-year corporate espionage and for hacking into an array of US industries, including aviation, telecommunications, pharmaceutical, automotive, satellite, cloud-computing and networking-support, banking, finance, biotechnology and health companies. The Chinese also hacked several government entities, including the Navy, the Lawrence Berkeley National Laboratory, NASA's Goddard Space Flight Center, and NASA's Jet Propulsion Laboratory. In

China Stealing US Technology

Intelligence Services
Non-Traditional Agents
Administrative Reviews
Joint Ventures
How China loots US tech
Research Partnerships
Mergers & Acquisitions
Academic Collaboration
Front Companies

Source: USTR, FBI, CIA, DoD

announcing the indictments, the US Deputy Attorney General, Rod Rosenstein, said, "This is outright cheating and theft, and it gives China an unfair advantage at the expense of law-abiding businesses and countries that follow the international rules in return for the privilege of participating in the global economic system." He added that "More than 90% of the department's cases against espionage in the past seven years involved China." Echoing similar sentiments, the FBI Director Christopher Wray said, "China's goal, simply put, is to replace the US as the world's leading superpower, and they're using illegal methods to get there."

China also steals US intellectual property through non-traditional information-collecting agents. These individuals are Chinese nationals or Chinese Americans. For instance, in 2011, the FBI uncovered some Chinese operatives who went to Iowa fields, dug up and stole special seeds from DuPont Pioneer and Monsanto, and tried to ship them back to China to help a Chinese company. The operatives fled the country but one of them was arrested and in 2016 pleaded guilty for his crime. This Chinese man had lived in the US for nearly 20 years, was a US permanent resident, and his children were US citizens. Talk about biting the hand that feeds you! In another case, two Chinese "tourists" were indicted in 2018 for conspiring to steal rice seeds to be used in medicine and drugs. The US company that was targeted, Ventria Bioscience, had spent tens of millions of dollars developing the intellectual property behind these rice seeds. These Chinese visitors were helped by two Chinese nationals who worked in the US: one worked for Ventria and was sentenced to 10 years' imprisonment, and another worked at the US Department of Agriculture's Dale Bumpers National Rice Research Center and was sentenced to one year in prison. And in another case, in 2018, a former Apple employee, a Chinese national, was arrested at San Jose International airport as he was preparing to board a flight to China on the charge of stealing driverless car secrets for a Chinese startup in Guangzhou that he was to join.

Another way that China has used for decades to steal US technology is through joint ventures. China forces US firms, and firms from other advanced countries, seeking entry into the Chinese market to form joint ventures with Chinese companies and transfer technology to them, with the aim of these local companies stealing the secrets of the foreign companies and eventually directly competing against them.

Another way that China underhandedly snatches US technology is through mergers and acquisitions, and equity investments. China targets key companies in critical high-tech areas and then buys them or buys stakes in them. China uses its state-owned enterprises, private companies, and venture capital firms to accomplish this goal. And the Chinese use every single maneuver they can think of to accomplish their goal, such as by swooping on US high-tech companies in financial difficulties and scooping them in bankruptcy courts. In 2018, US senator Cornyn said that China had "weaponized" its investments in America "in order to vacuum up US industrial capabilities from American companies." Tsinghua Unigroup, controlled of course by the Chinese government, tried to buy US memory-chip maker Micron for $23 billion and Western Digital for $3.8 billion when they were in difficulty, but thankfully failed. However, it did manage to snap up other US and European chip companies. More importantly, it found a willing sap partner in Intel, a company led of late by bean counters, "suits" that seem to only care about making a buck. Tsinghua Unigroup is working with Intel on the critical technologies of 5G and NAND chips, and will Sinicize Intel the way that China did to countless other US companies. Intel's IP will be ripped off, and the company will eventually be driven to ruin or irrelevance by the Chinese swamping of the market with cheap subsidized products.

Another way that China steals US technology is through front companies that pose as legitimate private businesses. The Chinese government uses US naturalized citizens of Chinese origin and private companies to get stealthy access to Western technology. For example, Canyon Bridge Capital Partners, a private equity firm headed by a US citizen born in China and whose financing according to Reuters could be traced back to China's State Council, tried to acquire Lattice Semiconductor Corporation, a US manufacturer of high-performance programmable logic devices, but thankfully the US found out about China's intentions and blocked the attempt. Canyon Bridge then acquired British chipmaker Imagination Technologies.

Another way that China steals US technology is through academic collaboration and research partnerships. For this purpose, China uses students, scientists, engineers, and businessmen. For example, in 2018, one Chinese student, who studied at a university in Chicago and even enlisted in the US Army reserves to become a US citizen, was arrested for attempting to help China recruit American scientists and engineers, some of whom worked in the defense industry.

And another way that China steals US technology is through its administrative review process that foreign firms have to go through in order to operate in China. Thus, when a US tech company wants to establish or expand its business in China, it must go through administrative reviews where it's required to disclose trade secrets to review panels, panels that share this vital information with competing Chinese companies. China also forces US companies seeking to do business in China to license technologies to Chinese entities on non-market based terms that favor Chinese recipients.

China uses all these ways to steal trade secrets that can help it narrow the technology gap with the West. The trade secrets that China has stolen took US and Western companies years and hundreds of billions of dollars of research and development. These stolen secrets allow the Chinese to build competitive, state-of-the-art products at a fraction of the cost of Western firms. For example, China has become a major global player in solar-panel, wind-turbine, and nuclear technologies through such theft of Western intellectual property.

Thus, China hurts Western economies not only by stealing valuable trade secrets, but also by then using those secrets to compete against Western companies and sell similar products at cut-rate prices that force those victimized Western companies to lay off workers, relocate overseas, or even go bankrupt. This double whammy of China stealing intellectual property and then dumping products in the West has wreaked havoc on the US economy, especially manufacturing.

And as expected, Chinese leaders always deny any wrongdoing. No matter how damning the evidence of their culpability is, they always blatantly lie and deny responsibility. And they continue lying. Thus, in 2015, on a visit to the US, Chinese president Xi Jinxing declared, "The Chinese government will not in whatever form engage in commercial theft." This pledge to refrain from hacking the US for trade secrets and intellectual property was just another example of Chinese deception. Indeed, in late 2018, then Attorney General Jeff Sessions said, "Chinese economic espionage against the United States has been increasing — and it has been increasing rapidly."

Speaking of Chinese espionage, the head of the FBI's counterintelligence division, Bill Priestap, told the Senate Judiciary Committee in December 2018 that "Every rock we turn over, every time we looked for it, it's not only there, it's worse than we anticipated."

China's corporate espionage shows that it can never be trusted. With respect to Xi's pledge not to hack, FBI sources revealed in 2018 that the Chinese had over the previous four years hacked the Marriott hotel chain and collected personal details of roughly 500 million guests. And not only did China target the US, but it also attacked the UK, Australia, New Zealand, Canada, Germany, Sweden, Finland, Norway, Denmark, the Netherlands, Poland and Japan.

Such deceit is symptomatic of modern China's zeitgeist of innate corruption. In China, there's what's called the "Original Sin," an expression that refers to how the great majority of today's rich Chinese got their wealth through corruption. This notion of original sin also applies to the Chinese government and companies. The likes of Alibaba and Xiaomi got their start by blatantly ripping off Western intellectual property rights. Alibaba and its Taobao e-tailer started their businesses and got rich by selling counterfeit and knockoff merchandise. And they still do while unashamedly pretending otherwise. Jack Ma, the founder and head of Alibaba, even acknowledged in a speech in 2016 that the fakes are often of "better quality, better prices than the real products, the real names." Xiaomi started out by selling phones that could only be described as crap, with screens so blurry that one could barely read them. And then it went on its Apple-robbing spree with the full help of the Chinese government. And after amassing great riches using these despicable methods, these Chinese companies have the audacity of going global and even listing in the US, all with the warm welcome of the utterly brain-dead American and Western leaders. This is pure money laundering. It's like the US accepting the drug cartel as a bona fide business and allowing it to keep all its ill-gotten riches. It's like the US welcoming Al Capone with open arms instead of prosecuting him. This is America, the land of what Trump correctly called the "Stupid leaders." All American leaders care about is making money for themselves and their buddies. Even so-called American conservatives and ultra-nationalists such as former US Congress House Speakers, senate leaders, presidential contenders, and US Secretaries of State have joined lobbying firms that help the despicable regime of China basically rape America. Incidentally, Trump also alluded to this raping of America by China.

And this raping of America continues to this day, as piracy of US products is still rampant in China among individuals, companies, government organizations, and schools. Chinese schools' intranets are chockfull of bootlegged US software, movies, TV shows, music and e-books. One need only go to any university, universities in China are owned by the government except for a handful of minor ones, and surf its Intranet. One will surely be shocked by the sheer huge magnitude of piracy in China. On such school intranets, one can find thousands of Hollywood movies and TV shows. One can find almost any music tune, whether it's rock, pop, rap, classical or whatever genre. One can find all types of e-books from Prentice Hall, Wiley and all the major publishers. And one can find all the popular software from Microsoft, Adobe, Apple, Oracle, Autodesk and others. As an example of such software piracy, the Business Software Alliance estimated that 70% of new PC software installed in China during 2015 was unlicensed, its value totaling almost nine billion US dollars.

Bootlegged DVDs and CDs are also brazenly peddled

in shops, online by e-tailers, and on the street by hawkers accosting passers-by at many places such as shopping areas and subway stations. An American movie DVD, which in the US can cost about $20, can be had for about $1 in China. US software, which can cost hundreds or thousands of dollars in the US, can also be had for $1!

Such piracy continues in China with the connivance of Chinese officials, who are only too happy to stick it to Uncle Sam. For example, while piracy is officially illegal in China, one can find shops selling bootlegged DVDs everywhere in China, even in trendy areas of Beijing like Sanlitun. The shops stay in business with the help of officials who receive some kickbacks in return. Whenever there's an impending inspection or crackdown due to some complaint from a US or Western entity, the officials alert the shop owners, who simply remove the DVDs from the shelves for a few days to let things calm down. In Beijing, such cat-and-mouse tactics happen regularly, and make a mockery of China's repeated pronouncements that it actively combats piracy.

A quick math, by examining just the segment of China's population with a college education, can reveal the enormity of the losses that Chinese piracy of digital content has inflicted on the US economy. The digital content on the computers of such people usually costs them nothing, at most a few dollars, since it's easily and freely downloaded or bought as bootlegged DVDs. And yet, this content is very valuable. First, the operating system is most likely Microsoft Windows, which is worth at least $100. Second, Microsoft Office, especially Word, is as ubiquitous as Windows. This software is worth at least $100. Third, Photoshop is wildly popular in China, both for professionals and casual users. Since this program is gotten for free, it's usually acquired as part of Adobe Creative Suite, which is worth at least $1,000. Fourth,

Chinese computer users have all sorts of other programs from US software companies, such as utilities, applications, and games, and these miscellaneous programs can add up to thousands of dollars, but to which a conservative estimate of $1,000 can be assigned. Fifth, there are American movies, which are very popular since Chinese movies are bush-league by comparison. Assuming that over the years, only a couple of hundred such movies were pirated and that each movie is worth $15, the total comes to $3,000. Then, there are the e-books, such as textbooks and novels, which can easily amount to thousands of dollars, and to which one can assume a conservative figure of $1,000. And finally, there's American music that's also very popular in China. Assuming a low estimate of 1,000 songs per computer since it's free music after all, and $1 per song, the total comes to about $1,000. Thus, a conservative estimate of the pirated digital content on the computer of a Chinese with a college education can easily top $7,000. This is a very reasonable estimate since some programs that are used on Chinese campuses, such as Autodesk Maya and SPSS, can cost thousands of dollars each. Assuming there are about 100 million Chinese with a college education, a fair estimate since according to China this number will balloon to 195 million in 2020, and assuming a piracy rate of 75%, the amount of pirated computer digital content can easily top $500 billion dollars. This is money that the Chinese, with the full support of their government, have unjustly deprived the US economy of. The US Government, if it had any guts, could use this money and punitive damages to cancel its Chinese debt.

Besides piracy, almost any product can be counterfeited in China. The list of counterfeit goods is unbelievably large and includes toiletries such as soap, shampoo and toothpaste, cosmetics, beverages such as beer, soft drinks and purified water, bicycles, motorcycles, cars (yes, this happened), shoes, clothing, jewelry, electronic products, food, and many other goods.

Counterfeit goods of sports brands like Nike and Adidas, clothes brands like Abercrombie & Fitch and North Face, luxury brands like Gucci and LV can be had on the cheap at many shopping places and online. Gucci was so fed up with Alibaba dragging its feet and allowing counterfeit products to continue to be listed on its online stores that in 2015 it filed a suit in a New York court. Of course, Gucci could not sue Alibaba in China and expect to win. Such a suit would be dead on arrival.

Knockoffs are also a big business in China. Many Chinese coffee shops design their logos à la Starbucks, with the familiar circular design and colors. Chinese food and beverage companies design their packaging to resemble that of US companies. One soft-drink company called Feicheng Kela designed its cola bottles to look exactly like those of Coca-Cola. Chinese car companies also sport logo designs that look very similar to foreign ones like BMW, Audi, and Toyota. Even stores aren't immune from knockoffs in China, as some stores have been built to look like exact replicas of those of Apple, Wal-Mart, Ikea, Starbucks, McDonald's, and KFC, inside and out. In the case of Apple, many such fake stores have sprouted in cities like Shenzhen and Kunming, and look every bit as Apple, from the iconic white logos to the employees dressed in blue T-shirts emblazoned with the Apple logo. They even take pre-orders for new iPhones. In one such counterfeit Apple store, the employees themselves believed they were working in a genuine Apple store. If even the employees can be duped, then unsuspecting customers can be forgiven for shopping in these places and thinking it's the real deal.

Copying in China knows no limit. Even services aren't

Chinese "Ingenuity"

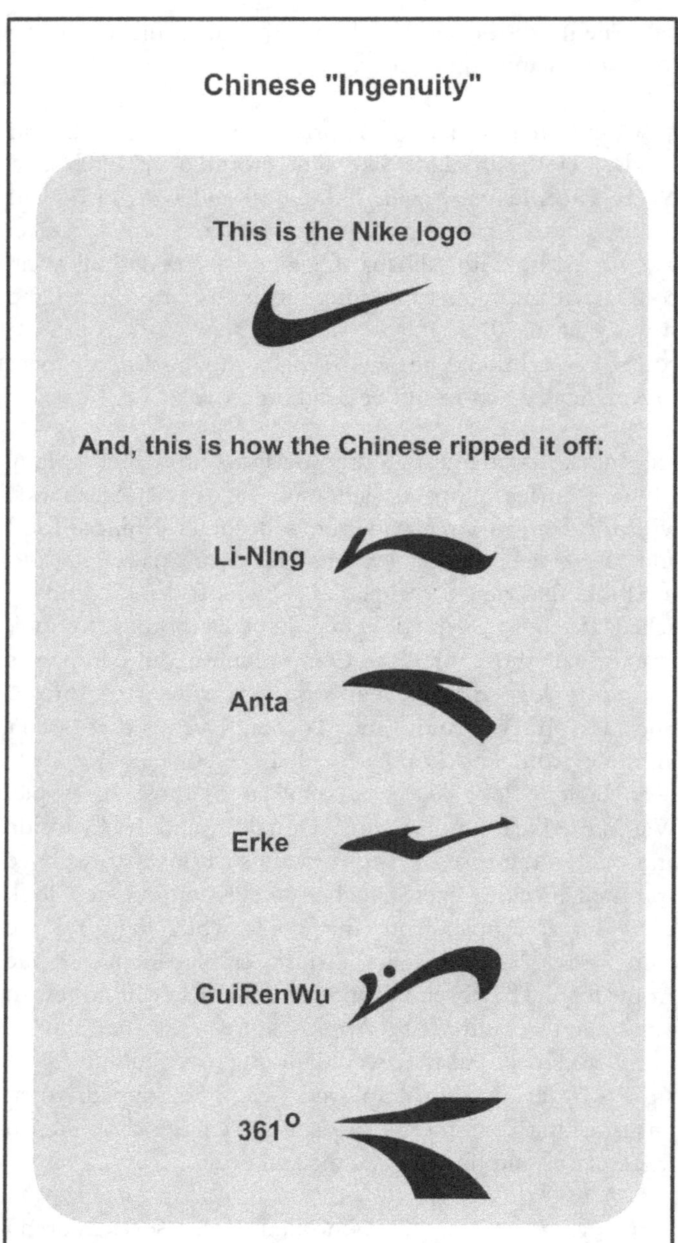

immune. Years ago, China had no police emergency service, and then it came up with one. Guess what! You dial 119.

This flagrant Chinese theft of US assets has been going on for decades. When China was weak, its argument was that piracy and counterfeiting were propping up its fragile economy, and cracking down on them would not only bring economic ruin but also social upheaval. Somehow the West went along with that logic in the hope that later on China would clean up its act and play by the rules. However, after China built up its powerful economy, it only paid lip service to Western complaints. This is to be expected of China, a country built on deceit. China now knows that it's in the catbird seat, that it can keep on ripping off the US and the West, and that it can hush them just by dangling the allure of its huge market.

China playing the West along

China has been playing the naïve and innately weak West along for decades. All along, Western countries have been aware of China's wrongdoings, and yet didn't stand up forcefully to them. Somehow the mirage of access to the huge Chinese market and the false hope that China would mend its ways and play by the rules totally paralyzed the West. China has been robbing the West blind, and yet the latter has been an out-and-out pushover. The Chinese aren't exactly super smart in business; it's just that they found in the West a willing patsy.

A perfect example of how China played the West along is how China kept an undervalued currency for many years in order to help its exports and build a strong economy at the expense of the West. This strategy worked wonderfully for China as its economy has now become the biggest in

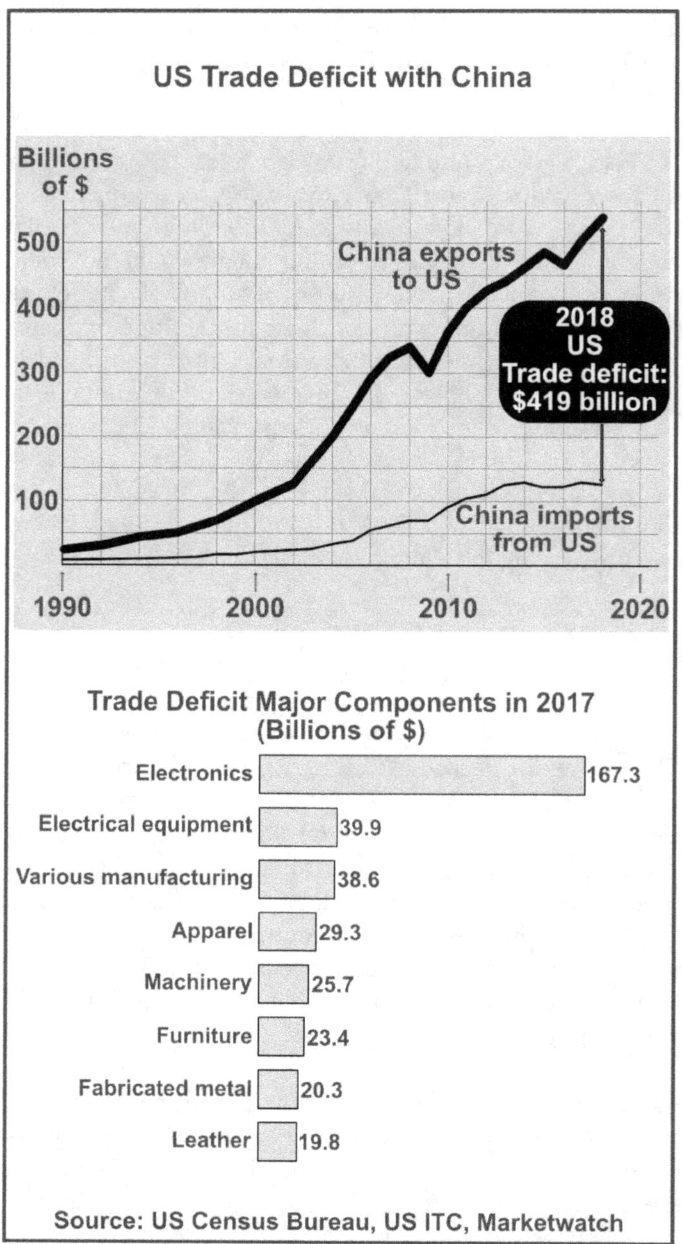
US Trade Deficit with China
Billions
of $
500
400
300
200
100
China exports
to US
2018
US
Trade deficit:
$419 billion
China imports
from US
1990
2000
2010
2020
Trade Deficit Major Components in 2017
(Billions of $)
Electronics 167.3
Electrical equipment 39.9
Various manufacturing 38.6
Apparel 29.3
Machinery 25.7
Furniture 23.4
Fabricated metal 20.3
Leather 19.8
Source: US Census Bureau, US ITC, Marketwatch

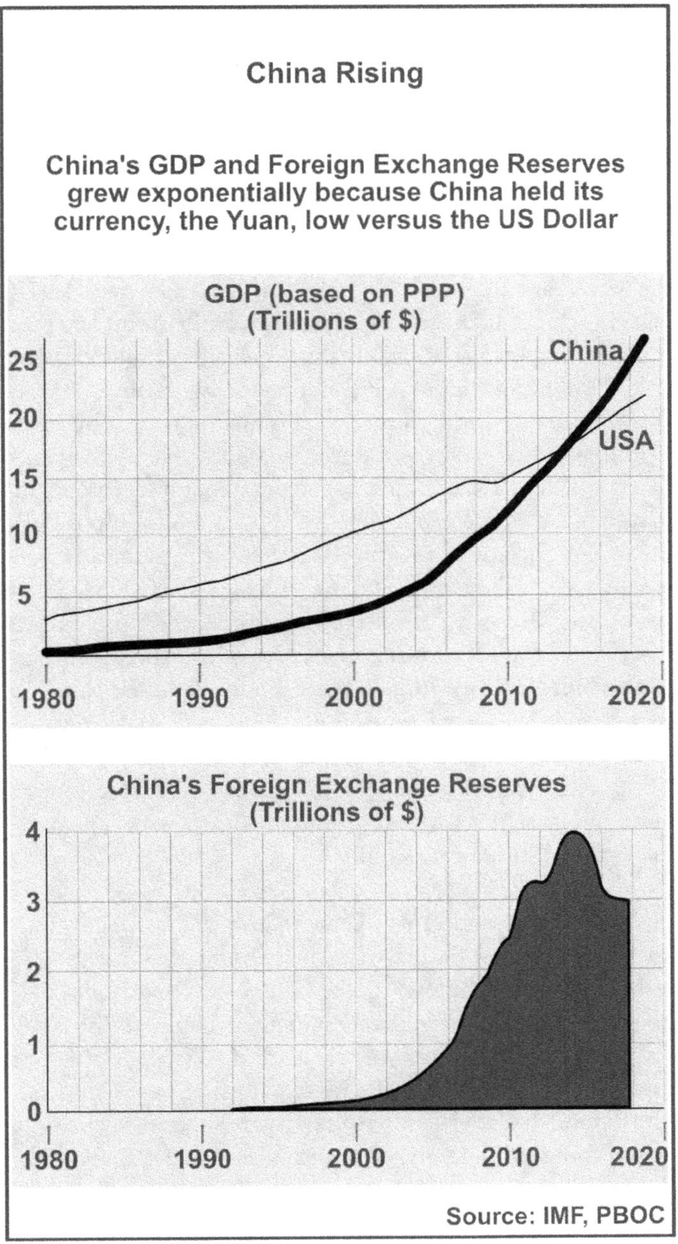

China Rising

China's GDP and Foreign Exchange Reserves grew exponentially because China held its currency, the Yuan, low versus the US Dollar

GDP (based on PPP)
(Trillions of $)
China
USA
25
20
15
10
5
1980
1990
2000
2010
2020

China's Foreign Exchange Reserves
(Trillions of $)
4
3
2
1
0
1980
1990
2000
2010
2020

Source: IMF, PBOC

the world according to some estimates, and so strong that there's now pressure on its currency, the Yuan, to grow stronger. So, China now correctly argues that it's not a currency manipulator, but that's after decades of currency manipulation! That currency manipulation wrecked US manufacturing. According to a report by the Economic Policy Institute, the US lost almost 3 million jobs, most in manufacturing, as a result of the US-China trade deficit in the ten years between 2001 and 2011. And what do US leaders do? Huff and puff, holler and thunder, and threaten or promise to label China a currency manipulator, and then do nothing! This happened with the Clinton, Bush, Obama and Trump administrations. President Trump shouted to no end during his presidential campaign that he would label China a currency manipulator on his first day in office. And yet, he didn't. Not only did he break his promise to the American people, but after meeting the Chinese president he even started profusely showering China with love and admiration. Who knows why; maybe it's because, as reported in The Guardian, soon after Trump took office, China granted him 38 trademarks in record time, trademarks for spas, massage parlors, golf clubs, hotels, shops, and even escort services. China also granted trademarks to Trump's daughter on the same day that the Chinese president dined with Trump at the latter's Florida mansion.

Such manipulation of Western leaders has been going on for decades. For instance, from time to time the US wakes up to Chinese malfeasance in trade and US politicians go up in arms and start their habitual display of discontent and threats of retaliation. These politicians throw everything but the kitchen sink at China by threatening to label it a currency manipulator, accusing it of dumping, threatening it with higher tariffs, threatening to take it to the WTO, and showing discontent in a myriad of other ways. So guess what China does! Right when the storm of discontent is brewing and raging in America, China sends a big shopping delegation to America to buy billions of dollars worth of US goods. The delegation targets key areas and places, such as the home states of the president and key congressmen. And hallelujah, the storm abates and everything between China and the US becomes hunky-dory again, at least until the next storm.

China was even able to manipulate the "hawkish" Trump. The case of ZTE, the Chinese networking-gear and smartphone maker, illustrates how China played Trump like a fool. The US intelligence community had for a long time warned about ZTE's ties to the Chinese government. ZTE had been fined for contravening US sanctions against Iran and North Korea. The Pentagon banned ZTE phones because the devices posed a security risk. And the Trump administration at first ordered a seven-year halt in American shipments of computer microchips and software that are at the heart of most of ZTE's telecommunications gear. However, China knew how to play the venal Trump. It got one of its state-owned companies to sign to build an Indonesian project that would include a Trump-branded hotel and golf course. And voila! Days later, the White House Fool tweeted that he was ordering his Commerce Department to immediately rectify the sanctions against ZTE by tweeting on May 13, 2018, "President Xi of China, and I, are working together to give massive Chinese phone company, ZTE, a way to get back into business, fast. Too many jobs in China lost. Commerce Department has been instructed to get it done!" This guy sounded like he was a defender of China at the expense of America. He became the latest American leader to kowtow to China.

In response to Trump's about-face, one of his Republican colleagues, Senator Rubio of Florida, said about the Chinese, "They are basically conducting an all-out assault to steal what we've already developed and use it as the baseline for their development so they can supplant us as the leader in the most important technologies of the 21st century."

Such Chinese manipulation also happens to Western companies. A perfect example is that of Microsoft. For many years, this company, whose Windows and Office software is used on basically all computers in China, generated less revenue in China than in a small country like the Netherlands. According to the words of its former CEO Ballmer, in 2011, Microsoft's revenue in China was 5% of its revenue in the US even though computer sales in the two countries were basically equal. Everyone knew that the huge lost revenue was due to piracy. And yet Microsoft continued doing business in China as usual for years and kept trying to please the Chinese government, all in the hope that someday things would change and China would start acting lawfully. China of course knew how to placate Microsoft and other foreign companies, so from time to time the Chinese police would orchestrate some phony dog-and-pony show for the Western media during which they burn, crush or steamroll seized pirated goods, like software and movie DVDs. Microsoft kept losing billions of dollars of revenue each year in China, all due to China's reprehensible inaction in combatting blatant and rampant piracy. And then in 2014, to add insult to injury, the Chinese government decided to investigate Microsoft for monopoly practices!

China played Microsoft along beautifully and milked it of billions of dollars. In 2018, Ballmer told Fox Business that, when he left Microsoft in 2015, 90% of Chinese companies were using Windows, but only 1% were paying for it, thus, costing Microsoft $10 billion or more in profit. In fact, in 2015, more than 97% of PCs in China were running Windows.

Another US company that China has played for years is Facebook. In 2018, Facebook's venture in Zhejiang province was pulled by the Chinese government, again dealing a big blow to Facebook's plans to establish a toehold in China. Facebook's CEO is just another moronic American business leader who thinks he can charm his way into China. He learned Chinese and is always cozying up to Chinese leaders. These guys give him all kinds of false hope by meeting up with him and posing with him in cheerful photo ops. But all they're doing is playing him like a fool, just as they've done with countless other American CEOs. Facebook is still blocked in China while China gives time to its own companies to grow and obviate the need for Facebook or any other American company.

Western companies' CEOs hear of a billion-consumer market and go, "Wow, that's the greatest opportunity ever!" But they sooner or later find out that in the end it was all a mirage or a minefield. Foreign car companies, such as GM and Ford, establishing joint ventures in China have had to share valuable and hard-gotten technology with their Chinese counterparts. Software companies Microsoft and Adobe have been robbed blind. IT company Cisco's code was stolen by the now formidable Chinese competitor, Huawei. Google was chased out by blocking its services and slowing them down, even though it was light-years ahead of the local rival, Baidu. Credit card companies Visa and Master Card were shut out for the benefit of their Chinese rival, UnionPay. Uber was forced to sell off to its Chinese competitor. And Apple was forced to hand over the operation of its cloud services in China to a Chinese company in a move to comply with China's anti-foreign cybersecurity law enacted in June 2017, which requires that data belonging to Chinese citizens and organizations must not only be stored within China, but also be stored in data centers and networks that are operated by local Chinese companies.

All such alarm signals notwithstanding, Western businesses still flock to China as the holy grail of investment. Take the example of the Chinese car manufacturer BYD auto! This company had the audacity to design its logo as an almost exact replica of the BMW logo. Indeed, the BMW logo has a circular design, and ditto for the BYD logo. The BMW logo has an outer black circle, ditto for BYD. BMW has its name written in white on the black circle, ditto for BYD. BMW's inner circle has two colors, white and blue, and guess what, ditto for BYD! This case plainly illustrates the Chinese total disregard of business ethics. But wait! Surprise, surprise, this Chinese company is backed by America's most famous investment guru, who praised the founder of BYD as one of the greatest minds around!

What Western leaders and companies fail to realize or are afraid to acknowledge is that the Chinese market is not a level playing field and the Chinese government is not a fair arbiter. According to the Heritage Foundation's 2016 Index of Economic Freedom worldwide, China ranks an appalling 140th in the protection of property rights, and 152nd in investment freedom. The Chinese government's main focus is to help Chinese companies develop and grow until they can push their foreign counterparts out or marginalize them. That is why the government insists on technology transfer in many major business deals, there are limits on the percentage of foreign ownership, there are limits on investment sectors, there are limits on capital outflow, the government is always propping up local companies with subsidies and policies, there are unfair tariffs on imports, Western corporate secrets are hacked and stolen by the Chinese, and so on. As for unfair business practices by Chinese companies, the Chinese government turns a blind eye. For Western complaints, the

Chinese government only gives lip service.

Thus, it should come as no surprise that Chinese companies, public and private, owe allegiance to the Chinese government, and have CPC committees. Heck, even foreign companies in China have CPC committees. According to Bloomberg in 2018, 70% of the 106,000 foreign firms operating in China had party committees. Even Jack Ma, the famous head of Alibaba, is a member of the CPC. Chinese companies may be listed overseas and pretend transparency and governance according to international standards, but they are the arm of the Chinese government, and are always at the ready to serve it. And of course, as stated previously, this is a two-way relationship. The Chinese government has their back and supports them at the expense of foreign counterparts. And support means dependable financial support and favorable policies. For example, mega deals like carmaker Geely's 2010 purchase of Volvo Cars and appliance manufacturer Midea's 2016 acquisition of German robotics maker Kuka were bankrolled by the Chinese government. And in 2018, the Chinese government blocked Qualcomm's $44 billion bid for NXP Semiconductors, even though eight other regulators around the world approved it, so as to weaken Qualcomm and allow the Chinese companies Huawei and ZTE to lead the 5G revolution.

Maybe Western leaders and businesses have realized that when it comes to doing business in China, that country and its companies always win and there's no point in challenging them. Chinese companies, and not just state-owned enterprises, have the full and unshakable support of their government. The Chinese government uses its regulatory power and courts to collude with Chinese companies against their foreign counterparts. Western companies, especially the American ones, can never count on such vital support from their governments.

Thus, a company like Apple, Inc., whose designs have been blatantly copied by its Chinese competitors Xiaomi and Huawei, doesn't dare sue them for fear of antagonizing the Chinese government. Apple sued the Korean company Samsung for years and for many design-copying infractions, even small details like round corners. However, Apple just had to sit and take it while the Chinese companies like Huawei and others blatantly copied the iPhone. For example, in late 2018, Lenovo released a new smartphone, the P30, that's a brazen rip-off of the iPhone X. It's similar in size, had a notch on the screen, had a vertical camera, and even its default wallpaper was similar to Apple's!

China uses many tools to bring Western companies to their knees. Thus, if a foreign company dares to challenge China, China may delay the certification of its products, put pressure on its Chinese suppliers and partners, investigate it for business infractions such as monopoly, disrupt or block its services, create work strikes in its supply factories, disrupt its supply chain, leave it out of the public procurement, unleash its courts against it, and even use the media against it. No wonder Western companies have been satisfied with any crumbs they could get from doing business in China.

China's success at playing the West along for such a long time, and the West's tepid protests have emboldened the Chinese into continuing their nefarious practices. As is their custom when they sense weakness, the Chinese have been ruthlessly taking full advantage of the West by continuing to engage in rampant piracy, cunning currency manipulation, extensive dumping, and prohibitive protectionism, such as by subsidizing their enterprises and adopting anti-competitive regulations. China persists in such unfair trade practices because it knows that not only the West lacks the resolve to push back significantly, but

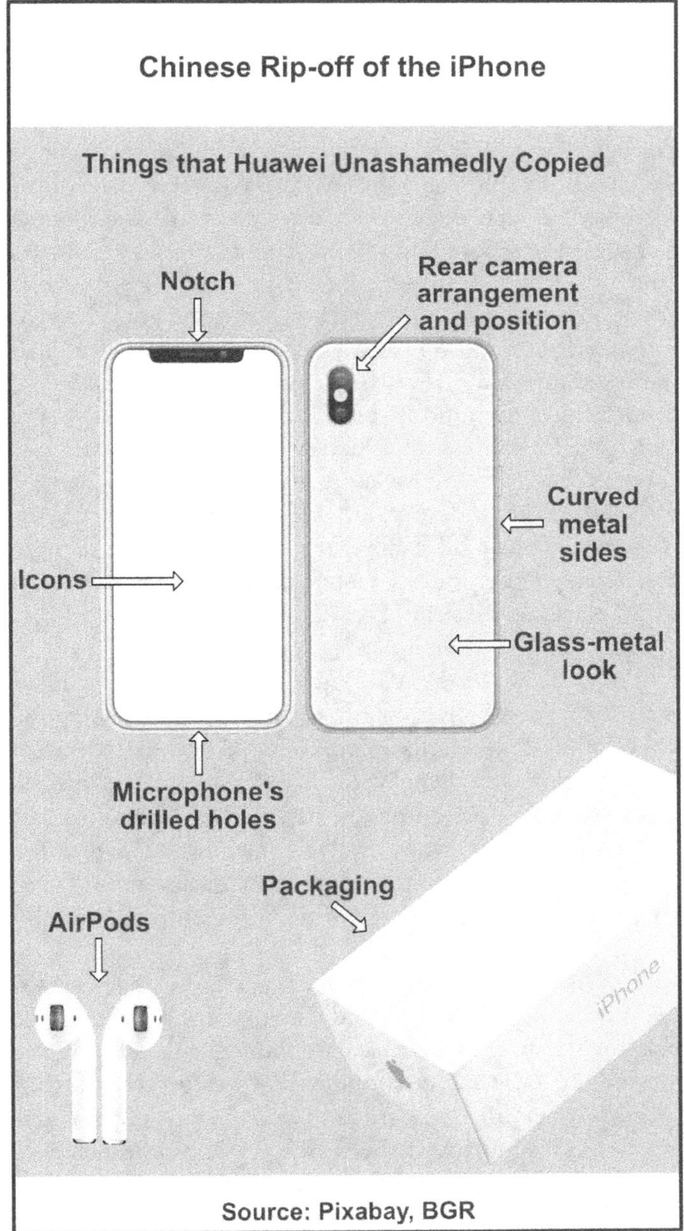

Chinese Rip-off of the iPhone
Things that Huawei Unashamedly Copied
Notch
Rear camera arrangement and position
Icons
Curved metal sides
Glass-metal look
Microphone's drilled holes
Packaging
AirPods
iPhone
Source: Pixabay, BGR

also that time is on its side. Indeed, China's economic might is growing exponentially, and its economic leverage to bully other countries will only get stronger. Also, when countries do complain to the WTO about China's unfair practices, the WTO may take years before rendering judgment. By the time the WTO takes action or some agreement is reached, China will have already caused great damage and rendered any WTO verdict or agreement too little too late. For example, when China passed a rule about a decade ago that mandated that wind turbines sold in China be made up largely of local components, that policy compelled major international manufacturers of wind turbines to not only relocate to China, but also more damaging to share their valuable technology with Chinese companies. Years later, when China was forced to get rid of that policy because of the outcry among many countries, China still came out a winner for the damage was already done. Indeed, China emerged as the dominant world player in the field of wind turbines.

China has used the WTO to advance its development at the expense of other countries. Indeed, since joining the WTO in 2001, China has played the US and the West like fools by not complying with WTO rules to disclose its subsidies, which are known to be massive. China finances its companies in many ways, including state-directed lending, direct investments, tax breaks and local government incentives.

A perfect case study that illustrates how China played the West along for so long and emerged a winner is that of Huawei. Huawei, which used to be a lightweight in the networking field, is now the world's largest vendor of telecom network infrastructure and soon the biggest smartphone company in the world. As with other Chinese companies, it relied on economic espionage and support from the government to realize its goal. In its early days,

Huawei survived by copying competitors' code and offering cut-rate low-level products. And it counted on a cash cow of unlimited funds, the Chinese government, which bought its products and also provided billions of dollars of credit to finance Huawei's deals around the world. Using such vital support and draconian work conditions that can only be described as Gulagish, Huawei shot to the top of world rankings. And China continues to support Huawei and other Chinese companies to the detriment of foreign companies and in contravention of WTO rules. For example, China sets the lion share of about three quarters of its mobile infrastructure market to Huawei and other Chinese companies like ZTE, while leaving a few crumbs for Western companies to fight over.

This Chinese policy has wrecked the US manufacturing industry in the telecommunications infrastructure sector. America's main manufacturer in this sector, Lucent, had to merge with its French counterpart Alacatel to stay alive. That merger didn't help and Alcatel-Lucent had to sell itself to Nokia. Another Western manufacturer in this field, Ericsson, had to cut it workforce by thousands of people. And the future still looks bleak for these telecom manufacturers. Indeed, whereas in the West, these Western companies have to struggle with economic cycles and downturns, Huawei and other Chinese manufacturers know that the Chinese government is always there to purchase their equipment and to actively support them both domestically and abroad.

And the impertinence of the Chinese towards the West keeps reaching new heights of insolence. Thus, while restricting its market to foreign investors, China unashamedly asks trading partners like the US and the EU to recognize it as a market economy. And while it keeps gobbling up foreign companies and assets, it severely restricts foreigners from doing the same in

China. Germany's economy minister exasperatedly chided China saying, "If you want to invest in other parts of the world, you can't block those countries from investing in your own."

The brazen attitude of the Chinese is not just confined to its politicians. Its nouveau-riche and parvenu business people are just as shameless. Their most famous business guy, a fellow who calls himself Jack Ma, came to the US to meet newly-elected US President Trump and promised to help the US create a million jobs. This is the guy who heads Alibaba and Taobao, or T-Mall, the outfits that got their start and amassed their riches by selling counterfeit merchandise!

And finally, another way that China has taken advantage of the West relates to environmental protection. Indeed, while China keeps polluting and raping our planet on an unprecedented scale, it has succeeded in getting developed countries to shoulder most of the responsibility for reducing the world's pollution.

The China deception syndrome

Faced with the overwhelming abundance of evidence from thousands of cases describing Chinese malfeasance, one could be forgiven for thinking that deception is in the DNA of the Chinese. China is after all the country of the *Art of War*, the masterpiece on deception in war, and business too, for the Chinese conduct business like war. Modern Chinese have taken deception to a new level, that of open and brazen lying and cheating.

Chinese lying starts at the top of their leadership. Speaking at the World Economic Forum in Davos in 2017, Chinese President Xi Jinping said, "Countries should refrain from pursuing their own interests at the expense of others." What baloney! So unashamedly and blatantly lying directly to the face of everyone! This is the same Xi Jinping who pledged in 2015 at the White House that China would stop economic cyber espionage, and yet China never stopped hacking the computer networks of US companies to access their sensitive commercial information and trade secrets.

Another example of Chinese lying is that according to the USTR report on China in 2018, China had on at least eight occasions since 2010 committed not to force US companies to transfer their technology to Chinese entities as a condition for market access, but that China continued with its unfair practice of coercing American companies to hand over valuable technology if they sought to enter the Chinese market. And to add insult to injury, not only had the US companies had to comply with China's demands, but they were also cowed by China into keeping silent about it. Indeed, according to that USTR report, the US companies have stated for more than a decade that they feared that they would face retaliation from China if they aired their grievances.

Another example of Chinese brazen lying was that in December 2017, President Trump accused China of not living up to the oil embargo on North Korea by saying that China was caught red-handed violating the embargo. China vehemently denied the charges. The US then showed satellite photos to prove how China had on dozens of occasions circumvented the embargo with ship-to-ship transfers in the Yellow Sea, and yet China as usual continued to lie about its involvement. The fact is that even if China pretends that it restricts trade with North Korea across their land border, China will continue using its thousands of boats and ships in the Yellow Sea to keep on trading with North Korea. In 2018, Reuters reported that according to South Korea, North Korea imported more than $640 million worth of luxury goods from China in 2017 in clear violation of the UN sanctions on the North Korean rogue regime.

And Chinese companies engage in the same tactics of deception and lying. In 2015, American Superconductor (AMSC) partnered with a Chinese company called Sinovel Windpower in order to access the Chinese wind-turbine market. And then as usual with the Chinese, Sinovel stabbed AMSC in the back. It bribed an AMSC employee and stole key wind-turbine technology. As a result AMSC saw its sales collapse, losing hundreds of millions of dollars, and had to lay off hundreds of employees. AMSC sued Sinovel in a US court and got a pittance back while Sinovel is now a world leader in wind turbines.

In 2018, China's state-controlled company Fujian Jinhua was indicted in the US for stealing US chipmaker Micron's trade secrets. According to the indictment, the stolen trade secrets for advanced DRAM chips were valued at up to $8.75 billion. And true to Chinese brazen attitude, Jinhua then filed for a number of patents based on the stolen secrets. And the crazy thing was that Jinhua then used the Chinese legal system, which of course takes its orders from the Chinese government and sides with Chinese companies, to block Micron from selling its DRAM products in China, claiming that Micron had infringed on its patents!!!!!

In 2016, Huawei uploaded a nice pic to its Google+ account, claiming that the pic was taken with its new smartphone at that time, the P9. However, as *AppleInsider* reported, the picture data clearly showed that the pic was taken with an expensive camera, the Canon 5D Mk. In 2018, Huawei produced a commercial showing the great pics taken by its Nova 3 smartphone. The problem, as

Engadget pointed out, was that the pics weren't taken by the said smartphone, but rather by a DSLR camera. Also in 2018, according to *Engadget* and AnandTech, Huawei cheated by ramping up its phones' performance whenever they detected the public versions of benchmarking apps, and cheated by huge margins, sometimes up to almost 50% higher than their normal operating benchmarks. And when confronted, Huawei said that it was common practice in China. Huawei said it had to cheat to compete against the other cheating Chinese companies! Also in 2018, the US Justice Department indicted Huawei for ripping off T-Mobile USA's phone-testing robot, *Tappy*. Prosecutors said that Huawei engineers secretly took photos of *Tappy*, and even stole a piece of the robot to try to replicate it. Commenting on the case, FBI Director Christopher Wray said, "In pursuit of their commercial ambitions, Huawei relies on dishonest business practices that contradict the economic principles that have allowed American companies and the United States to thrive." In fact, according to the US Justice Department, Huawei has a program that rewards employees for stealing data from other companies, with better bonuses based on how confidential the stolen information is.

And of course, not only Chinese leaders and companies lie and cheat, but also Chinese individuals and groups engage in such repugnant behavior. In 2018, *The Information* reported a major fraud case in China that targeted Apple. Chinese thieves bought or stole iPhones, and then removed valuable components from them, components such as CPUs that they sold on the black market. The thieves then replaced the components with fake parts, put the iPhones back together, and took them to Apple stores claiming that they were broken and needed to be replaced. Since the Apple employees couldn't readily see any tampering, as the iPhones couldn't even be turned on, they handed out replacement iPhones to the thieves who then resold them.

The Chinese engage in such deceptive tactics all over the world, even in the US. In 2019, two Chinese engineering students in Oregon were indicted for a similar scam against Apple. The two Chinese, working with their families and friends, imported thousands of fake iPhones from China to the US, and then conned Apple into trading them for legitimate ones.

China's debt diplomacy

China has not only played the developed countries, especially the West, like a fiddle and took full advantage of them, but it also has been conquering the rest of the world, especially poor countries, through huge investments that make the recipient countries economically overly dependent on China, a strategy that China leverages to further its economic, political and military interests around the world. China's lending practices are such that the affected poor countries get hooked on Chinese debt and wouldn't be able to repay it, thus placing them at the mercy of China. These Chinese predatory economics have been disastrous for some poor countries to the point of compromising their sovereignty. Indeed, as repayment, China demands control of their national strategic assets like ports, natural resources, or even territory.

The example of Sri Lanka very clearly illustrates the devastating consequences of falling for China's debt-trap diplomacy. China took advantage of the corrupt government of Sri Lanka and rushed in with huge and often economically questionable investments that left that country saddled with a crippling debt to China. Then, when Sri Lanka couldn't repay its debt, it was forced to grant China a 99-year lease on the strategic deep-sea port

China's Predatory Economics

Country

How it was forced to pay debt to China

Sri Lanka

Ceded control of the port of Hambantota to China for 99 years

Pakistan

Ceded control of the port of Gwadar to China for decades, and plans for a Chinese naval base in Jiwani

Kyrgyzstan

Ceded large chunk of its territory, which was annexed by China

Cambodia

Ceded to China the control of the whole coast, including the port of Sihanoukville, which has become a Chinese city, and the port of Koh Kong, which is being prepped for a Chinese naval base. Also acts as China's vassal in ASEAN

Djibouti

Allowed a Chinese military base on its territory, and is on way to ceding control of its main port

Greece

After China's takeover of Greece's biggest port, Piraeus, Greece acts as China's defender in the EU

Angola

More than half of its oil exports go to China to pay its debt

Ecuador

Half of its oil exports go to China to pay its debt

of Hambantota. In addition, Sri Lanka has been forced to spend about 80% of its government revenue paying down the China debt.

The consequences for poor countries that are recipient of Chinese investments can be even more disastrous. In 2011, Tajikistan conceded 1,158 square kilometers of its territory to China in exchange for debt relief. And in the case of Cambodia, China extracted the ultimate in debt repayment. Indeed, in exchange for investments, Cambodia became not only a vassal state of China, but truly a Chinese neo-colony.

Commenting on China's predatory economics around the world, US Vice President Mike Pence said in a speech in 2018 that China had chosen "economic aggression" against others, especially the US, and "debt diplomacy" to spread its influence by subjugating recipient nations.

The former US Secretary of State, Rex Tillerson, said, "China, as it does in emerging markets throughout the world, offers the appearance of an attractive path to development. But in reality, this often involves trading short-term gains for long-term dependency."

His replacement, the next US Secretary of State, Mike Pompeo, said in 2018 that "China shows up with bribes to senior leaders in countries in exchange for infrastructure projects that will harm the people of that nation," that "When China comes calling it's not always to the good of your citizens," and that "When the Chinese show up with deals that seem to be too good to be true it's often the case that they, in fact, are." Pompeo accused China of engaging in "predatory economics 101"and warned that "China has invested in ways that have left countries worse off." He noted that China has engaged in an "unprecedented level of larceny" of intellectual property, and added that China's recent claims of "openness and globalization" are "a joke."

The Chinese have been spreading their predatory economics to every corner of the world. In Africa, Chinese companies have turned the whole of Africa into a huge construction site for railways, highways, airports, ports, economic zones, industrial parks, power plants, hydroelectric dams, stadiums, government buildings, hospitals, military compounds, commercial buildings and so on. China has even built the African Union headquarters in Ethiopia, although it also bugged the building. According to the BBC, China is now the single largest financier of infrastructure in Africa, far surpassing the Asian Development Bank, the European Commission, the World Bank and the G8 countries combined.

Most African countries have become hooked on Chinese debt, sometimes to critical levels. According to the BBC, in 2017, 74% of Zambia's external debt was owed to China, and 77% of Djibouti's external debt was owed to China. According to the Financial Times, 50% of Angola's external debt was to China.

In the case of Zambia, there are presently at least 100,000 Chinese living in that country, according to The Diplomat. The country is so indebted to China that there are risks that it may have to hand over control of its strategic national assets, such as its power grid or airports, to China. The Chinese have become so powerful and influential in the country that the government appointed eight Chinese policemen into Zambia's Police Service, an act that raised a national outcry.

The crazy thing is that not only are the Chinese overburdening African countries with debt, but they have also brought their usual problems of corruption, crime, pollution, and ill manners to Africa. The Chinese look down on Africans, and in some cases insult them as monkeys. Some Chinese father babies with African women and then flee. Some Chinese don't allow African customers in their restaurants. Some Chinese treat their African workers like slaves. Some Chinese beat their employees for being lazy or shoot them for going on strike. The Chinese brought their prostitutes to Africa. The Chinese engaged in illegal mining, such as for gold. Some Chinese factory owners abscond and don't pay their African employees. Some Chinese illegally overstay in Africa. Some Chinese engage in online and phone scams. The Chinese pollute the environment by relocating polluting industries from China to Africa. The Chinese harm the ecosystem by engaging in illegal logging and poaching of endangered species. The Chinese deplete the fish stocks of African countries by illegal fishing. The Chinese have brought their corrupt ways to Africa by bribing officials and propping dictatorships. And the Chinese avoid paying taxes to African countries.

In Latin America, countries like Ecuador, Peru and Venezuela have become heavily indebted to China, and the Chinese continue their nonstop breakneck push into this area. China's forays in the Amazon basin are particularly alarming since that basin is a critical part of the world ecosystem. In their quest for natural resources, the Chinese have been destroying pristine swaths of the Amazon rain forest for their mining and drilling operations. The Chinese have also built dams there and are pushing to build an Amazonian railway from the Atlantic Ocean to the Pacific Ocean. In 2018, Brazil's new president, Jair Bolsonaro, warned against China's shopping spree in Brazil's energy, infrastructure, logistics, finance, mining, farming, and real estate, and said that "The Chinese are not buying in Brazil. They are buying Brazil." He was right. For example, in the energy sector, according to Reuters, one Chinese company, China Three Gorges, owns 17 hydropower plants and 11 wind farms in Brazil.

China is even trying to extend its nefarious presence in Oceania through its debt diplomacy. It has been investing in and loaning money to poor South Pacific island nations with the aim of bringing them under its control. In 2018, there were credible reports from US and Australian security experts that China approached Vanuatu about the possibility of opening a naval base there. The sneaky Chinese way was to first ask Vanuatu to allow its ships to sometimes dock there for repairs, and then when Vanuatu can't pay its debt, China will ask for a long-term lease to build a logistics or naval base.

China building a new world order

China is gradually putting a stranglehold on the world economy as it keeps growing at unprecedented rates. It's already the biggest economy in the world when measured by Purchasing-Power-Parity GDP. It's the world's largest merchandise trader. In 2017, it was the world's second largest receiver and provider of foreign direct investment. It's now not only a leader in traditional industries, but also a leading force in the industries of the future, such as IT and AI. China is the world's leader in energy production and consumption. Thus, when it comes to electricity generation, China's output eclipses that of the US, and is used to power its insatiable demand for the electrification of its urbanization drive and millions of factories. China produces and consumes around 60% of the world's cement, as evidenced by its phenomenal infrastructure buildup of new cities, skyscrapers, roads, highways, ports, and airports. China produces more than half of the world's output of steel, an incredible amount that not only is used in China's buildup but also is dumped around the world. China is the largest producer and consumer of coal, and

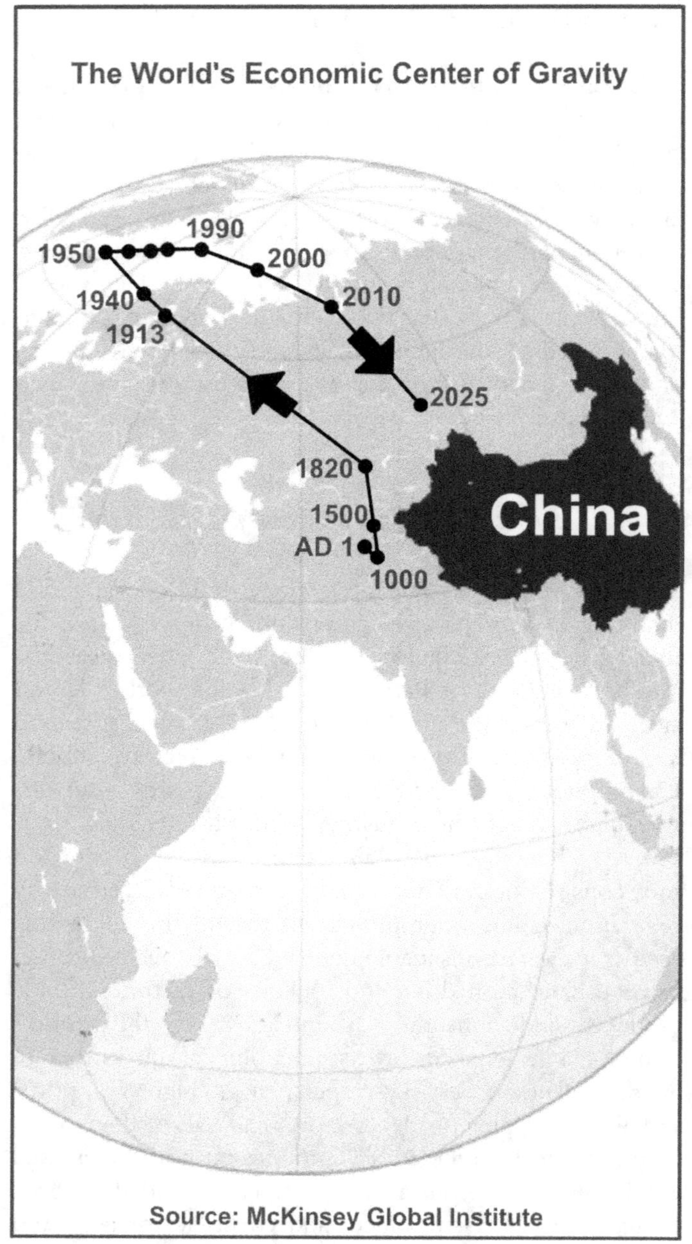

The World's Economic Center of Gravity
1990
1950
2000
1940
2010
1913
2025
1820
1500
AD 1
1000
China
Source: McKinsey Global Institute

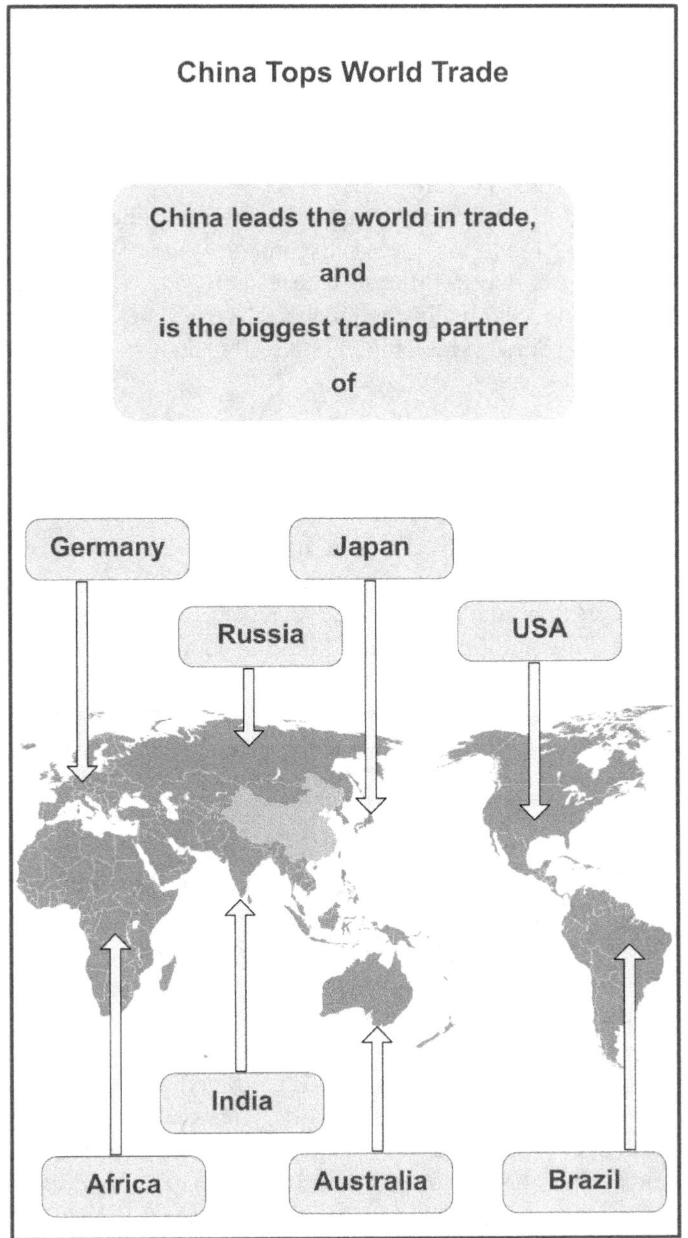
China Tops World Trade

China leads the world in trade,
and
is the biggest trading partner
of

Germany
Japan
Russia
USA
India
Africa
Australia
Brazil

consumes about half of the world's total. China is the largest importer of petroleum. And China is also the largest emitter of carbon dioxide—the most abundant of the anthropogenic greenhouse gases.

And now that China has developed such a mighty economy, it's not shy anymore about revealing its true intentions, those of global dominance and hegemony. China knows that in order to realize such goals, it needs to contain and eventually marginalize the present dominant power, the West. And China has already taken steps in this regard.

On the domestic front, China wants its firms to totally dominate the market and push out foreign firms, especially Western ones. Thus, China isn't satisfied that it's already the factory of the world and its policies have wreaked havoc on the manufacturing industries of the West; it also wants its manufacturing to be even more dominant. In 2015, China announced the "Made in China 2025" plan, which focuses on making China a leading manufacturing power in ten strategic sectors: rail, vehicles, shipping, aerospace, agriculture, power, materials, automation, biopharmaceuticals, and IT. Two key aspects of this plan are localization, with the goal of using mostly domestic content for core products, and market share, with the goal of Chinese companies totally dominating the domestic market. China wants to dominate these sectors as it has done with steel, aluminum, solar power, and wind power. The plan aims to raise domestic content of core components and materials from 40 percent by 2020 to 70 percent by 2025. The plan aims to achieve its goals through the continuation of China's protectionist measures of subsidies, indigenous standards, anti-competitive and restrictive policies, and government-backed investment funds. China has committed hundreds of billions of dollars in capital to this program to power the country to become

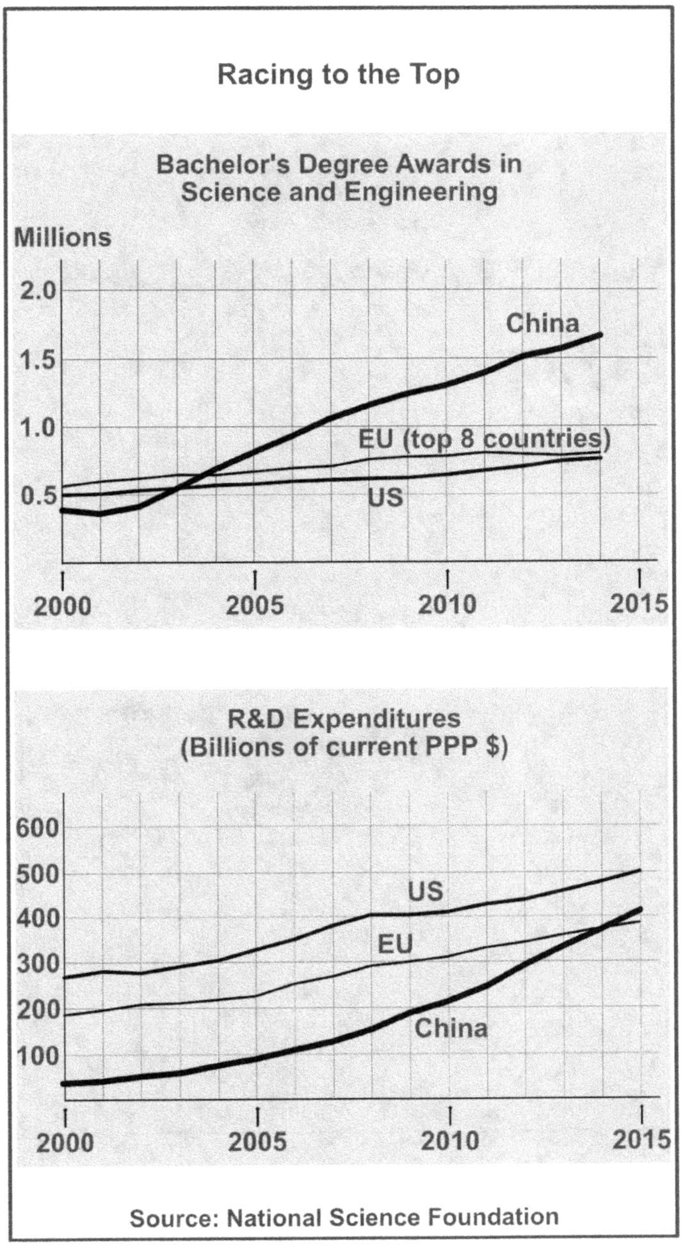

Racing to the Top
Bachelor's Degree Awards in
Science and Engineering
Millions
2.0
1.5
1.0
0.5
China
EU (top 8 countries)
US
2000
2005
2010
2015
R&D Expenditures
(Billions of current PPP $)
600
500
400
300
200
100
US
EU
China
2000
2005
2010
2015
Source: National Science Foundation

China Taking the Lead

Nations with the World's Most Powerful Computers (November 2017)

China	202
US	143
Japan	35
Germany	20
France	18
UK	15

Top 10 Most Powerful Supercomputers in the World (November 2017)

Rank	Name	Country	Performance
1	Sunway TaihuLight	China	93
2	Tianhe-2	China	34
3	Piz Daint	Switzerland	20
4	Gyoukyou	Japan	19
5	Titan	US	18
6	Sequoia	US	17
7	Trinity	US	14
8	Cori	US	14
9	Oakforest-PACS	Japan	14
10	K Computer	Japan	11

(Performance in petaflops)

Source: Top500

the world's technological superpower and dominant global economy. China is now already the world's largest exporter of high-tech products, and the 2025 plan will cement its world technological superpower status.

On the international front, China has already carried out policies and achieved steps to overtake the West and dominate the world. Thus, China has been using a checkbook diplomacy to not only attract the few remaining countries that still recognize Taiwan, but more importantly to wrestle countries all over the world from under the influence of the US and the West. Towards achieving this goal, China, under the leadership of Xi Jinping, launched in 2013 the "One Belt, One Road" initiative to build infrastructure and foster trade with countries near and far.

One Belt refers to the land bridge going from China all the way to Europe and encompassing Central Asia, West Asia, and the Middle East. And One Road refers to a maritime lane that includes coastal states from Southeast Asia all the way to Africa and Europe. Even Oceania is included in this initiative's One Road.

This initiative, now referred to as BRI or Belt and Road Initiative, aims to closely link countries in Asia, Europe, Africa and Oceania to China though huge and long-term investments in railways, roads, ports, energy systems, telecommunications networks, and other infrastructure. China is the Goliath of infrastructure, and there's always a great need for infrastructure around the world. China's strategy of course is to make its investments pay off in more than economic terms, and extend its influence to every corner of the world.

Africa is now pretty much in the Chinese sphere of influence. African countries like Sudan, South Sudan,

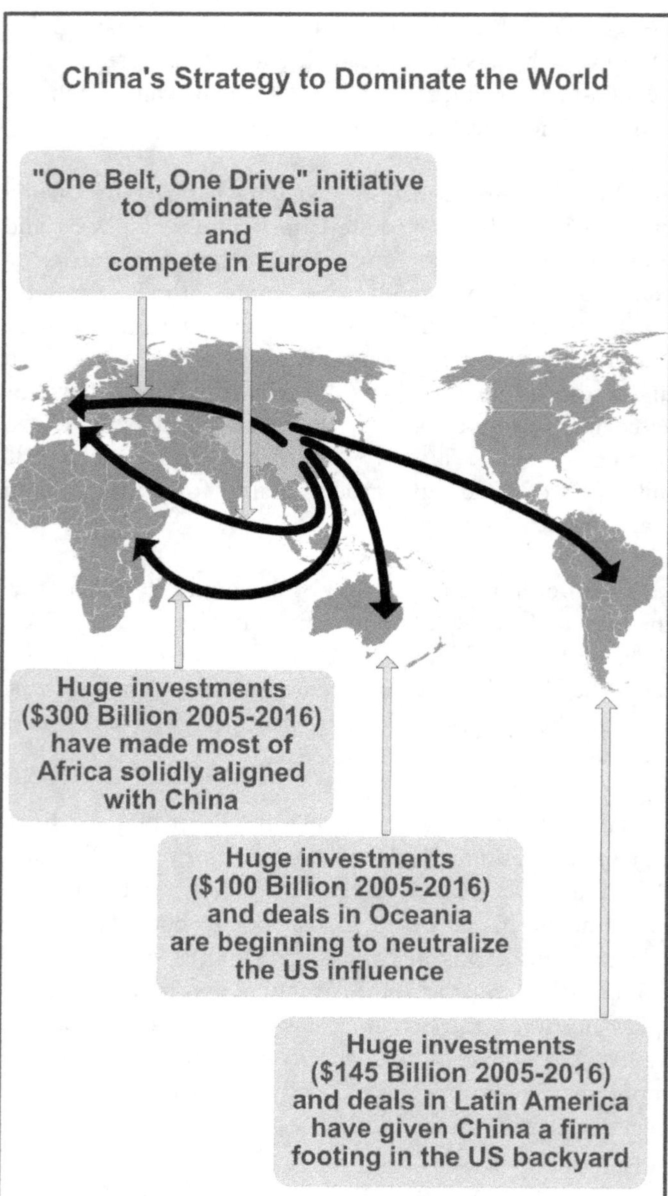
China's Strategy to Dominate the World

"One Belt, One Drive" initiative
to dominate Asia
and
compete in Europe

Huge investments
($300 Billion 2005-2016)
have made most of
Africa solidly aligned
with China

Huge investments
($100 Billion 2005-2016)
and deals in Oceania
are beginning to neutralize
the US influence

Huge investments
($145 Billion 2005-2016)
and deals in Latin America
have given China a firm
footing in the US backyard

Source: $ figures from China Global Investment Tracker

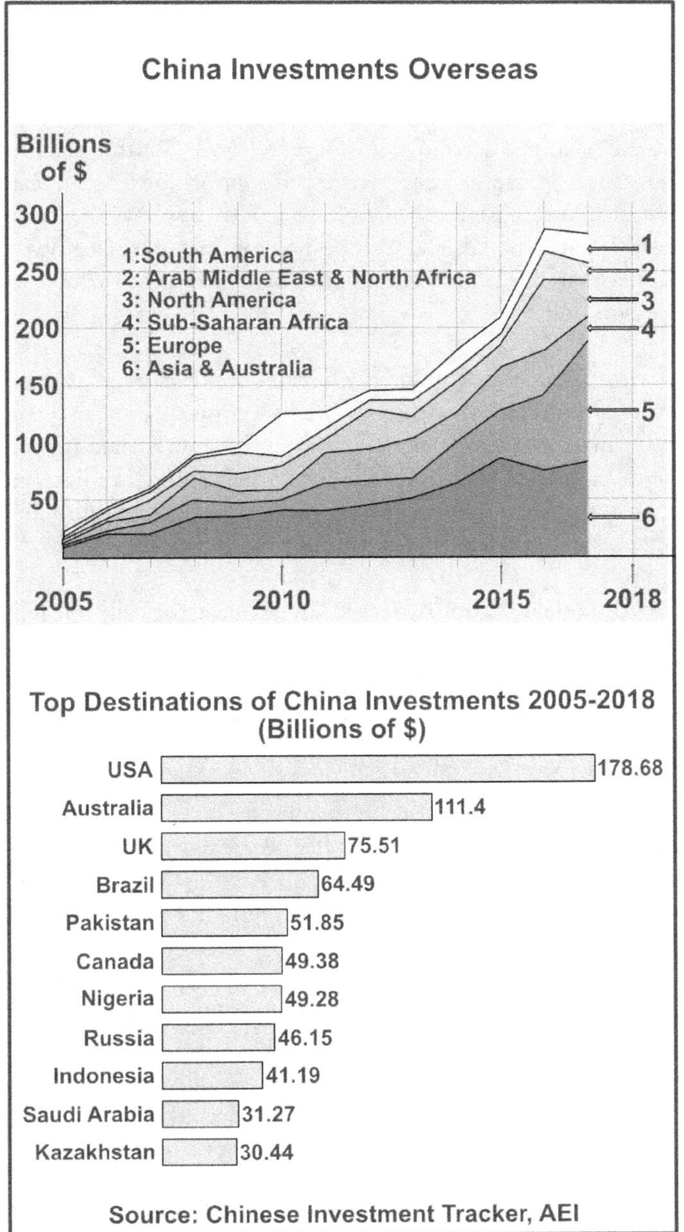
China Investments Overseas
Billions of $
300
250
200
150
100
50
1:South America
2: Arab Middle East & North Africa
3: North America
4: Sub-Saharan Africa
5: Europe
6: Asia & Australia
1
2
3
4
5
6
2005
2010
2015
2018
Top Destinations of China Investments 2005-2018
(Billions of $)
USA 178.68
Australia 111.4
UK 75.51
Brazil 64.49
Pakistan 51.85
Canada 49.38
Nigeria 49.28
Russia 46.15
Indonesia 41.19
Saudi Arabia 31.27
Kazakhstan 30.44
Source: Chinese Investment Tracker, AEI

Ethiopia, Angola, Tanzania, Algeria and many others have received billions of dollars in Chinese investments, and have adopted very close ties with Beijing.

In Asia, many countries in Central Asia, South Asia and Southeast Asia have received enormous Chinese investments, and many of these countries have become vassal states of China. Cambodia, for instance, is now a China satellite that strictly follows China's orders in foreign policy.

In Oceania, not only have small countries been swayed away from Taiwan with sizeable investments, but also the two main countries of Australia and New Zealand have been swamped with Chinese investments and immigrants that seriously undermine the two countries' traditionally unshakable relationships with the US and the West.

And even Latin America, an area historically closely linked to the US, has now started tilting toward China. Latin American countries like Brazil, Venezuela, Cuba, and Ecuador have received tens of billions of dollars in investments from China.

The fact is that when it comes to investments in the developing world, whether it's Africa, Asia or Latin America, China has already eclipsed the West, and is widening its lead. Such huge investments have allowed China to subjugate many countries by becoming their main trading partner and largest investor, such as in the case of Cambodia in Asia and Sudan in Africa.

Such huge investments have also allowed China to shape the world to its liking. Indeed, unlike the West, China doesn't condition its investments on improvements in human rights and governance. Thus, Chinese investments are more welcome in developing countries, many of which are dictatorships that are pariahs to the US and the West. China has no compunction about keeping these despicable regimes in power because it's one of them.

And China has not only exported its totalitarian practices, but also its inhumane labor practices. Thus, Chinese companies abroad often treat local workers like they treat Chinese workers back home. Chinese managers abroad expect local workers to work as slavishly as the Chinese in China, that is work for very low wages, work overtime all the time, and live in horrendous conditions. And even worse is that in many documented cases, Chinese managers beat and even shot with guns their local workers for various reasons, such as when the workers made mistakes, complained about the harsh working conditions, or went on strike. Chinese companies abroad also tend to bring their own Chinese workers, and in some projects the Chinese are either the majority or the total workforce.

In addition to its checkbook diplomacy to wean countries away from Western influence, China has also undertaken to fundamentally change the world's financial system. Not content with joining the present international financial institutions like the IMF, China has created or helped create banks that challenge the entrenched Western institutions that are the World Bank and the IMF. Thus, China has led the creation of the Asia Infrastructure Investment Bank, the Silk Road Fund, and the New Development Bank, which provides funding for the BRICS. At the same time, China has basically conned and bullied the IMF into accepting its currency, the Yuan, as a reserve currency, even though this currency is not fully convertible on the world market. The Yuan is now part of the IMF's Special Drawing Rights, making it the only emerging market currency in the basket. This is but one

Petroyuan Displacing the Petrodollar

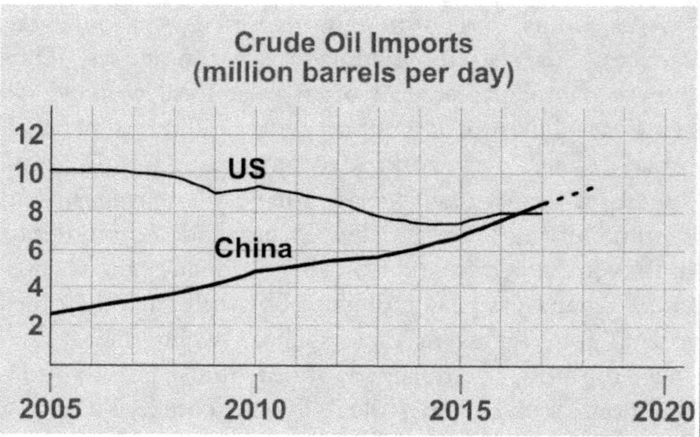

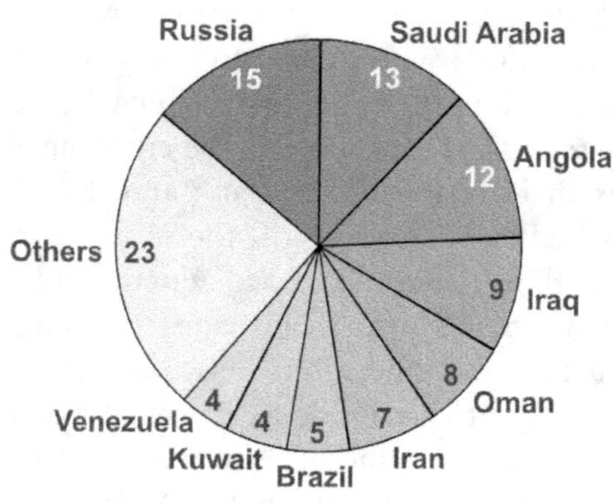

Source: EIA, DoD, China Customs

first step in China's drive to make the Yuan overtake the Dollar as the dominant world currency.

China's drive to overtake the West knows no limit, and the Chinese have taken their fight to Western countries' turf. Thus, Chinese companies have raided Western markets and gone on acquisition binges. They've been buying everything they could get their hands on, and the list includes hotels, entertainment venues, car companies, auto-supply companies, food companies, farms, electrical appliance companies, heavy machinery companies, high-tech companies such in robotics and semiconductors, football clubs, and more. They even tried to purchase the Chicago Stock Exchange.

While the US has been able to somehow control the Chinese invasion, Europe is a different story. Among their many conquests in the old continent, the Chinese have targeted ports and power grids. The most famous Chinese conquest is of course in Greece. China, through its state-owned COSCO, holds a controlling stake in the port of Piraeus. This port has become China's main gateway to Europe. And the funny thing is that the EU was the one that forced Greece to cede control of the port to China. And China's control of European ports doesn't stop in Greece. Over the last decade, and as part of China's Maritime Silk Road initiative to extend its influence, China has acquired stakes in more than a dozen other European ports in Italy, Spain, France, Belgium and the Netherlands.

As for power in Europe, China's China Three Gorges snapped up more than 20% of Portugal's power grid, again because the EU forced Portugal to sell off assets. The Chinese company committed to remaining a minority shareholder; however, true to the Chinese inherent practice of deception, this Chinese company is now trying to buy a majority stake. This company and other Chinese state-owned enterprises are vying, and are likely to succeed, to control the generation and distribution of power in Portugal. Besides Portugal, Chinese companies also control significant stakes in Italy's power grid, Greece's power grid, and the UK's gas network. In the UK, China also has a one-third stake in the Hinkley Point nuclear power plant, which will provide 7% of the nation's electricity needs when it comes online in 2025.

And the Chinese have gone further; they have also established a strong and permanent presence all over the world. Indeed, the Chinese have bought up or leased for decades millions of acres of land and farms around the world. In the US, the Chinese have been on a real-estate buying spree as they have acquired residential real-estate, commercial real-estate, warehouses, and hotels like the famous Waldorf Astoria in New York. Incidentally, this latter acquisition has made this landmark hotel, which used to be the residence of choice for US presidents visiting New York, off-limits to them for security reasons. The Chinese have become the largest foreign buyers of US property and have poured tens of billions of dollars in the US market. In Australia, the Chinese tried to buy that country's largest landholder and control 1.3% of that country's area! Fortunately, the Australians came to their senses and resisted that attempt. However, the Chinese have invaded Australia on an unprecedented scale and gobbled up huge amounts of real estate and farmland. In Canada, the Chinese control large real-estate holdings and keep snapping up more in key places like Toronto and Vancouver. And the crazy thing is that the Chinese have not been content with just buying up land around the world; they also have been building and trying to build whole Chinese cities and communities all over the world, including in the US.

In Italy's Prato, where an estimated 30,000 legal and

Han Hordes Swarming the World

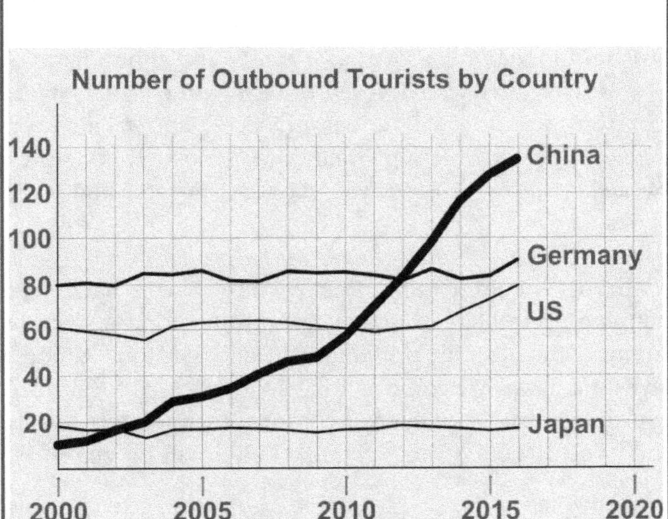

**The Chinese uncivilized manners,
around the world and in Sweden too,
led a Swedish news outlet
to mock them with this portrait**

Source: WTO, OECD, Svenska Nyheter

illegal Chinese immigrants live, the local Italians have accused the Chinese immigrants of bringing their usual uncivilized ways of piracy, tax evasion, unregistered businesses, money laundering, gang violence, drugs, prostitution, gambling, garbage, noise, and rude manners. The Italians have also accused the Chinese of bankrupting local business through unfair practices, and taking over whole areas to set up their own restaurants, stores, sweatshops, travel agencies, massage parlors, and even banks.

In 2019, commenting on how the Chinese have been popping up in huge numbers around the world and in his country, Brazil's vice-president Mourao said that Chinese investment was welcome as long as it followed local rules, explaining that "A Chinese company cannot arrive here and bring 100,000 Chinese people to work in Brazil."

Throughout the world, huge illicit financial flows from China have allowed corrupt Chinese to launder their ill-gotten riches, raised real estate prices in the recipient countries, and made life miserable for the locals. Australia, New Zealand and Canada have been heavily affected. Vancouver, the beautiful Canadian city, is now recognized internationally as a hub of Chinese money laundering. Chinese investors in Cambodia have been known to smuggle in literally boatloads of cash through the port of Sihanoukville, which has become basically a Chinese city. One Chinese brought in ten million dollars stuffed in mattresses that were shipped in through that port.

The Chinese are profiting of the West and weakening it in the process using every means possible. Now China has even become a major source of illegal drugs that have contributed to an opioid epidemic in the US. The Chinese produce synthetic drugs, such as Fentanyl and its derivatives, and conveniently ship them to the US via the

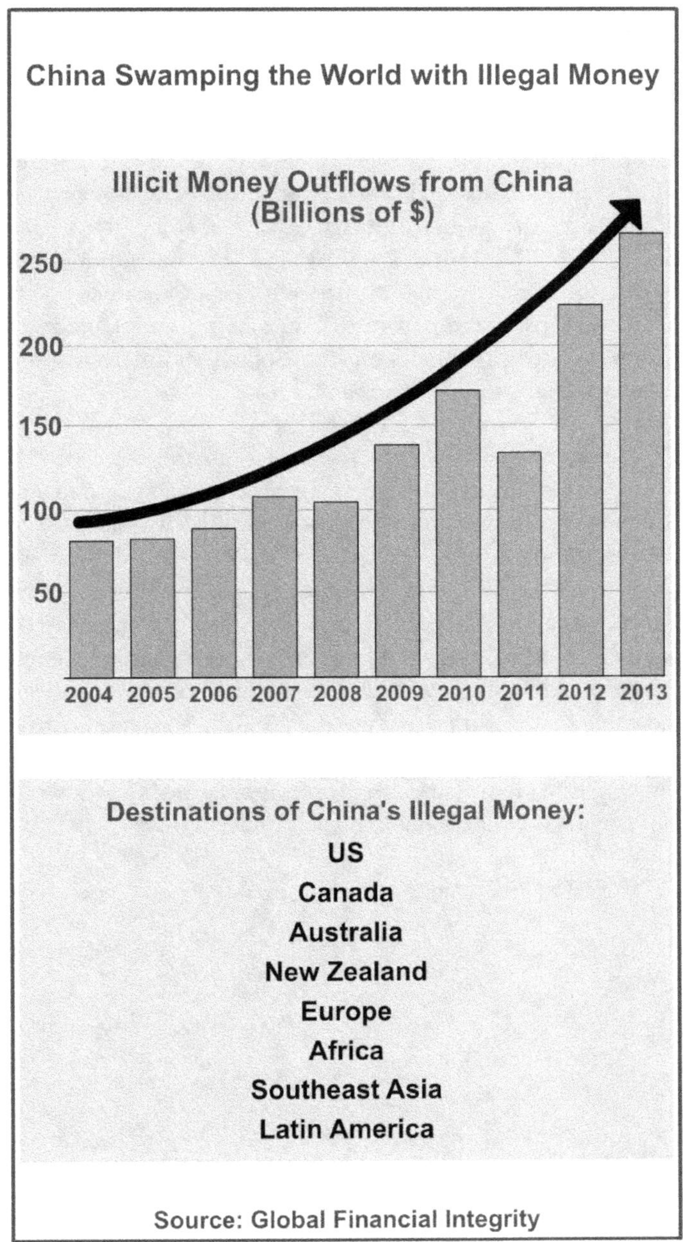

China Swamping the World with Illegal Money

Illicit Money Outflows from China
(Billions of $)

250
200
150
100
50

2004 2005 2006 2007 2008 2009 2010 2011 2012 2013

Destinations of China's Illegal Money:

US
Canada
Australia
New Zealand
Europe
Africa
Southeast Asia
Latin America

Source: Global Financial Integrity

postal system. According to US Government estimates, this fentanyl kills 100,000 Americans a year.

China has built up its mighty economy by robbing the West blind, and by ruthlessly taking advantage of the West's weaknesses. China is now well on its way to dominating the global economy and reshaping the world order. The Western ideals of fair business practices, respect of human rights, transparency of government, and protection of the environment are being supplanted by China's corrupt practices, abuse of human rights, totalitarianism, and environmental havoc.

The scourge of China's rise has been the bane of the West. Even the 2008 Great Recession was caused by China's rise, according to a report by CNBC. Indeed, at the beginning of the 2000s decade, the Fed slashed its funds rate to goose the US economy after the dot-com bubble, sparking a refinancing boom in the US and a growth in personal spending. This US spending binge fueled economic growth in China. However, the report indicates that during that time the Chinese stashed most of the money they got, half of their GDP, in low-interest savings, thus depressing long-term interest rates worldwide and fueling a US housing market bubble.

The China menace is upon the world.

3

ENVIRONMENT

China's breakneck drive to modernize itself, and its global activities of energy resources drilling, raw materials mining, logging, deforestation for farming, reckless dam building, large-scale infrastructure binge, war on wildlife, and illegal overfishing are wreaking unprecedented damage on our planet's ecosystems and biodiversity.

Today's Chinese truly have a problem living in harmony with nature. Wherever they have settled, in China or in other countries, they have congregated and quickly multiplied in great multitudes, and caused great harm to the environment. They consume the world resources at astronomical and unsustainable rates. They pollute in apocalyptic levels. They ravage wildlife. They build and build to no end, and pave over everything. They destroy natural habitats to erect concrete jungles. They destroy wetlands, rivers, lakes, mangroves, hills, and mountains to build, build, build. When they see a beautiful deserted dirt road or alley, they want to pave it over and jam it with traffic. When they see a quaint charming building or place, they want to raze it down and erect gaudy concrete monstrosities. When they see beaches, they want to build right on the sandy areas or dredge up the sand for more construction. When they see mangroves, they want to pour concrete and create more land for development. When they see lakes, they want to fill them up and develop real estate. When they see isthmuses, they want to build canals. When they see hills and mountains, the want to scar them or totally flatten them for quarries. When they see woods and forests, they want to cut them down for timber. When they see rivers, they want to dam them ad infinitum. When they see coastlines, they want to build deep-sea ports. And the list of Chinese destruction of the environment is endless.

No country has ever damaged our planet so rapidly, and on such a large scale.

China ravaging our planet

A United Nations Environment Program (UNEP) report warned that, "China's dramatic economic growth over the past few decades has increased demands for natural resources within and beyond the country itself in ways that are unprecedented in human history." Indeed, China keeps consuming mind-boggling amounts of materials, energy, and food, and is threatening our planet like no other country ever had. China has unleashed its unsophisticated nouveau riche and uncivilized hordes on the world in the name of trade and development, and in the process has caused great harm to our planet. The Chinese are gobbling up all kinds of resources, such as raw materials and food, at alarmingly unsustainable rates. One incredible example is that, according to the US Geological Survey, China consumed more concrete in the three years from 2011 to 2013 than the US did in all of the 20th century! And not only are the Chinese using up and depleting the world resources on an unprecedented scale,

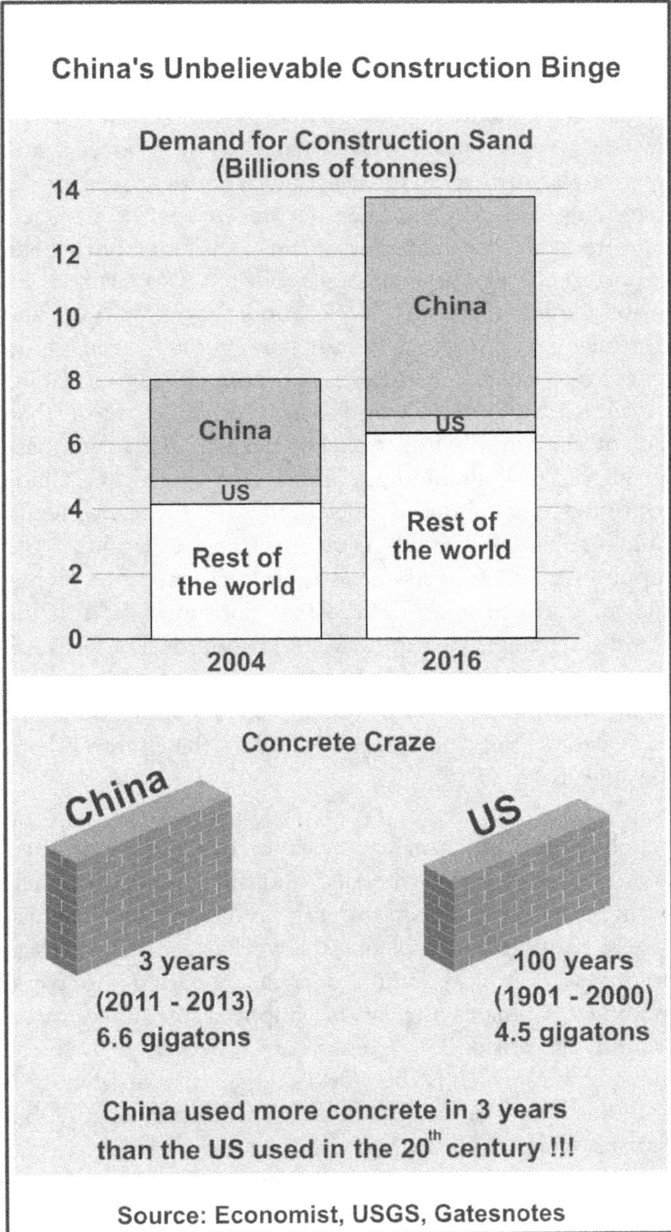

China's Unbelievable Construction Binge

Demand for Construction Sand
(Billions of tonnes)

14
12
10
8
6
4
2
0

China
US
Rest of
the world

China
US
Rest of
the world

2004
2016

Concrete Craze

China
US

3 years
(2011 - 2013)
6.6 gigatons

100 years
(1901 - 2000)
4.5 gigatons

China used more concrete in 3 years
than the US used in the 20th century !!!

Source: Economist, USGS, Gatesnotes

but they have also been recklessly causing great damage to the environment all over the world.

China's appetite for raw materials seems insatiable. Its own huge production of raw materials, such as coal and iron, isn't sufficient to keep its factories and plants humming, and so China has become the world's biggest importer of raw materials. China has not only been importing a lot of raw materials, but has also snapped up major mining assets in Africa, South America, Asia, and Australia. All these raw materials go into feeding a monstrous and inefficient economy. Thus, China consumes half of the world's coal and much more than half of the world's iron ore. For each of the major base metals of steel, aluminum, copper, zinc and nickel, China consumes half of the world's supply. In precious metals, China consumes about a quarter of the world's gold supply. And to feed its infrastructure construction frenzy and huge urbanization drive, China consumes 60% of the world's concrete, a figure that won't soon decline because, according to the South China Morning Post, China plans to move another 390 million people, a population that's equivalent to the whole of the US, from the countryside to the cities by 2030.

Chinese companies are scarring our planet in their insatiable quest for materials, and they go about their business with total disregard for the environment. Thus, they're harming and depleting the world's forests in Africa, Southeast Asia and Latin America. According to some estimates, China is the largest importer of stolen wood around the world. The Chinese are especially a threat to the Amazon, which is the world's largest terrestrial carbon sink and plays a critical role in regulating the global climate. China is destroying the Amazon and the lives of its indigenous people as the Amazon basin has become China's top supplier of commodities, including oil, iron,

China Gobbling up World Resources

Percent of World Consumption in 2014

54%	49%	60%
Aluminum	Coal	Concrete
48%	23%	40%
Copper	Gold	Lead
50%	46%	46%
Nickel	Steel	Zinc

- -

22%	31%	28%
Corn	Cotton	Meat
50%	30%	35%
Pork	Rice	Seafood

Source: OECD, FAO, IMF, USDA

copper, timber, soy, and beef. In Ecuador, Chinese copper and oil companies have secured huge forest tracts in the Amazon, and pursue their harmful mining and drilling despite the protests of the local tribes whose livelihoods have been shattered. These locals have no recourse for justice since the Ecuadorian government is totally in China's pocket because of the country's huge debt to China, and since the corruption is rife among Ecuadorian officials. In Suriname, which already had a sizable Chinese community, thousands more Chinese immigrants have descended on this Amazonian country. According to The Guardian, the Chinese now control 90% of that country's supermarkets and other stores. That country, known for its rampant corruption and crime, is now firmly in China's grip, and serves as a base for China to expand its influence in the region, and damage the Amazon. And in Brazil, China's financing and investments have led to the expansion of industrial agribusiness into remote, pristine rain forest areas of the Amazon.

China, which has 20% of the world's population but only 8% of its arable land, also has an insatiable need for food that domestic production can't satisfy. For example, China consumes about one third of the world's rice and half of the world's pork. Thus, China has turned to procuring food from overseas. However, the Chinese haven't just been importing food, but also have gone on an aggressive spree to acquire foreign food assets. Thus, they have bought foreign food companies, such as the big US pork company of Smithfield Foods, the world's largest pork producer. They bought the Swiss ag-tech company of Syngenta in their biggest-ever foreign acquisition for $43 billion. Syngenta is a world leader in advanced crop-protection products, such as insecticides and herbicides, and a top global producer of seeds. And the Chinese have been buying up huge farms in many places around the world, farms such as in Australia and New Zealand to raise cattle and sheep, and farms in Brazil and Argentina to grow soybeans and corn. In one case, China made a huge land lease agreement with the Ukraine to rent three million hectares of the latter's arable land, the equivalent of 5% of Ukraine's territory!

And China's run on the world's food supply extends to the sea. Indeed, China, with its huge population, its voracious appetite for all kinds of food including seafood, and the world's largest fleet of deep-sea fishing vessels that dwarfs that of any other country, has depleted fish stocks around the world. According to Bloomberg, China accounted for 35% of the world's seafood consumption in 2015.

The Chinese have not only depleted the fish stocks in their territorial waters, but they have also had a devastating impact on fishing waters around the world, especially near Africa, where governments are too weak and too corrupt to defend their territorial waters and exclusive economic zones. And the Chinese not only encroach on other countries' waters and steal their fish, but they also flout international rules by engaging in a destructive type of fishing called bottom-trawling, a practice where the net being dragged along the ocean floor scrapes up or kills any living thing in its path. The Chinese have of course shown their total disregard for environment protection whether in the air, on land, or in the sea. For example, in the South China Sea, they destroyed huge coral reefs in order to build artificial islands.

The Chinese, as is their usual nefarious practice, engage in many more illegal fishing activities around the world. Thus, they hide the whereabouts of their vessels by transmitting incorrect data about their location, they fly different flags to mask their vessels' identity, they change the names of their vessels, and they don't declare their catch. When the Chinese enter into agreements with other countries to fish in their waters, they, as expected, declare only a tiny portion of their catch, robbing the host countries of needed funds.

And the belligerent Chinese have become so brazen in their overseas poaching activities as to engage in fights with the coast guards of host countries that are fighting to safeguard their territorial waters, such as South Korea, Japan and Indonesia. Sometimes the Chinese boat captains are so aggressive as to ram those coast guard ships, forcing the latter to use drastic defensive measures, such as shooting the Chinese captains or sinking their boats. These aggressive activities by the Chinese fishing vessels have the full support of the Chinese government, which not only gives them substantial subsidies but also always takes their side in any dispute. For example, in one case where the Indonesian coast guard caught a Chinese boat illegally fishing near its Natuna Islands and tried to tow it to shore, China dispatched its huge coast guard ships and forced the Indonesian coast guard to free the Chinese boat. And later, China demanded the immediate release of its detained fishermen by claiming that the fishing grounds near Indonesia's Natuna Islands have historically belonged to China!

The fact is that the Chinese fishing armada doubles as a maritime militia that China uses to enforce its political claims in its near seas. Thus, China supports and encourages its fishing vessels to roam the Yellow Sea, the East China Sea and the South China Sea all the way to the doorsteps of countries like Japan, the Philippines, Vietnam, and Malaysia, and encroach on their sovereignty. In 1978, a flotilla of hundreds of Chinese fishing vessels approached the Senkaku Islands of Japan to challenge Japan's claim to them. One of Japan's nightmarish scenarios would be if one day China decides to take control of those islands using hundreds of its fishing ships. Japan would be rendered powerless. In July 2019, the US State Department condemned China for "the use of maritime militia to intimidate, coerce, and threaten other nations."

Another way that China uses its fishing vessels is for maritime surveillance of foreign navies. Indeed, the Chinese military provides Chinese fishing vessels with satellite navigation units that use China's global satellite navigation system, Beidou. Beidou, the Chinese word for the Big Dipper, is China's answer to the US GPS. Beidou became operational in the Asia-Pacific region in 2012, and is slated for completion in 2020 when it will have a constellation of 35 satellites to provide global coverage. The Chinese military is already using Beidou, such as for precision-guided missiles. One way that Beidou is different from the US GPS is that it's a two-way messaging platform, and China's maritime militia of fishing boats use this capability to send messages about the location of foreign navy vessels.

China polluting our planet

Besides gobbling up the world's raw materials and endangering the planet's food supply, the newly prosperous Chinese have been recklessly polluting our planet. Air pollution in China has reached apocalyptic levels, as China has been the world's largest emitter of greenhouse gases for more than a decade now. Air pollution levels in Chinese cities like Beijing are tens of times worse than what's deemed safe by the World Health Organization. The smog can be so thick as to close roads, airports, schools, and businesses. China's air pollution also affects the neighboring countries of South Korea and Japan through smog and acid rain, and has even reached

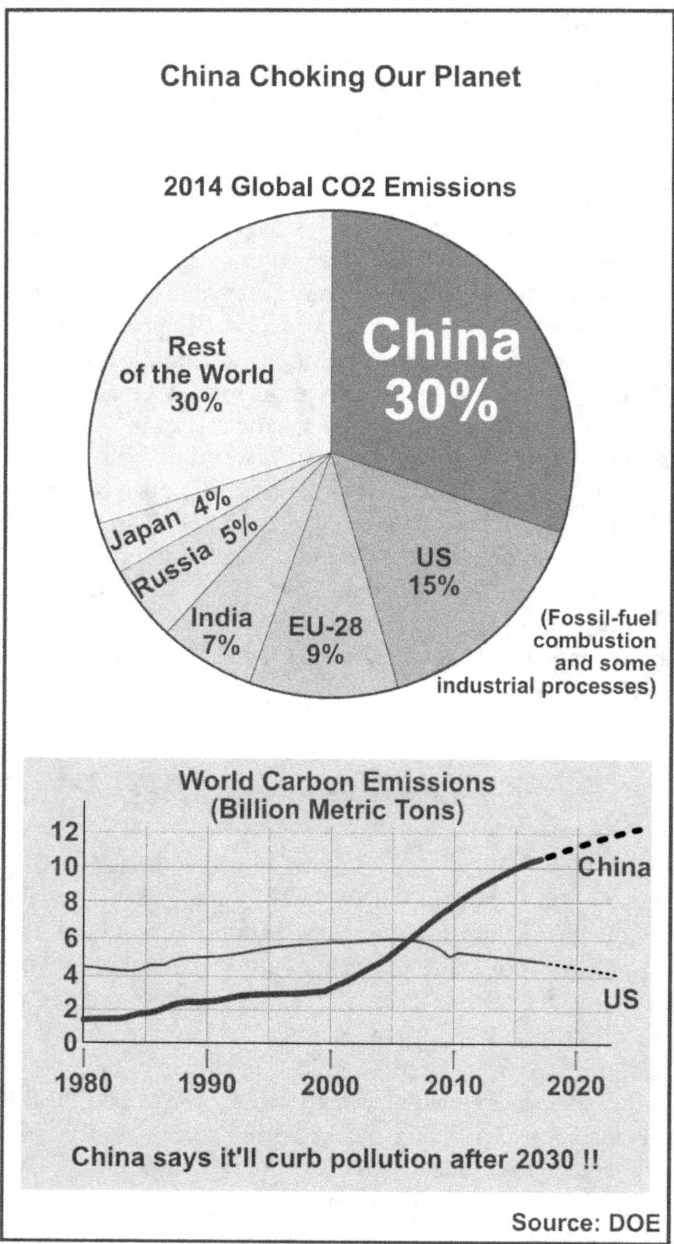
China Choking Our Planet
2014 Global CO2 Emissions
China
30%
Rest
of the World
30%
Japan 4%
Russia 5%
India
7%
EU-28
9%
US
15%
(Fossil-fuel
combustion
and some
industrial processes)
World Carbon Emissions
(Billion Metric Tons)
12
10
8
6
4
2
0
China
US
1980
1990
2000
2010
2020
China says it'll curb pollution after 2030 !!
Source: DOE

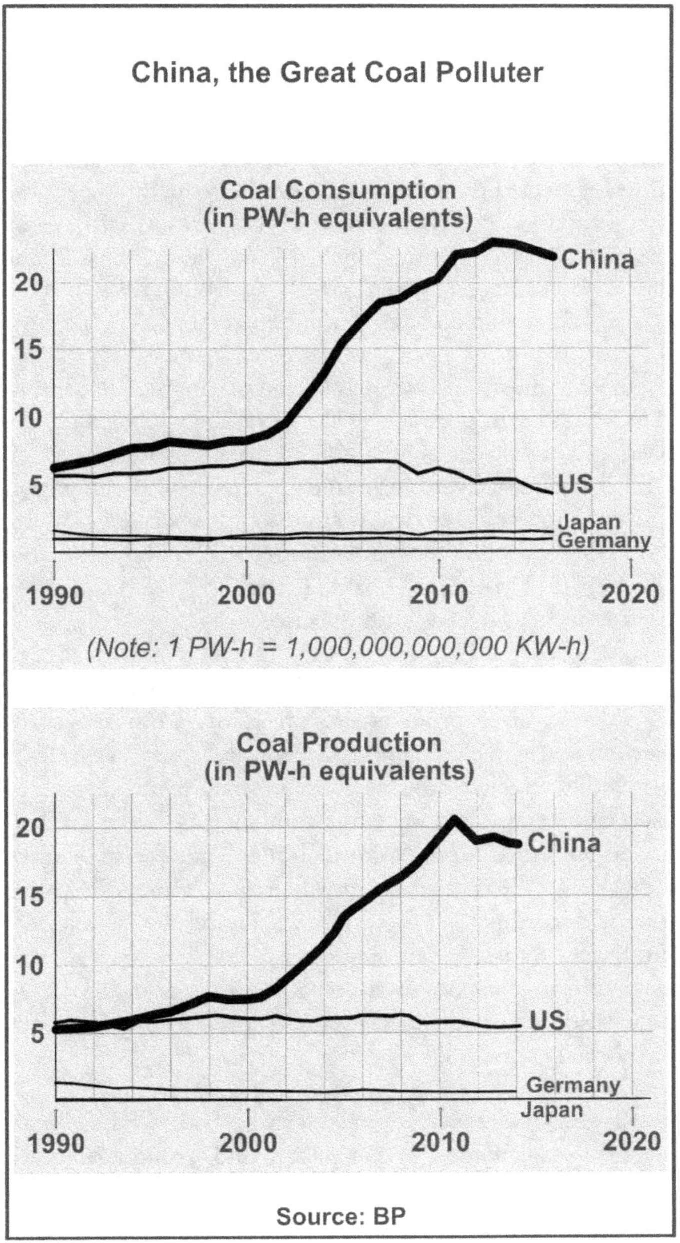
China, the Great Coal Polluter
Coal Consumption
(in PW-h equivalents)
20
15
10
5
China
US
Japan
Germany
1990
2000
2010
2020
(Note: 1 PW-h = 1,000,000,000,000 KW-h)
Coal Production
(in PW-h equivalents)
20
15
10
5
China
US
Germany
Japan
1990
2000
2010
2020
Source: BP

western US states, such as California.

Despite these calamities, China still hasn't totally committed itself to significant steps that could save our planet from dangerous global warming. Indeed, while China agreed to the Paris Treaty on the reduction of global warming, it only volunteered to halt the growth of its greenhouse gas emissions by 2030! By then, China, by far the world's largest greenhouse gas polluter, will have caused irreparable damage to our planet.

In the meantime, China keeps playing its deception games that harm our planet. For example, while China has been cutting down a little on its polluting industries by reducing coal consumption and increasing the generation of electricity from renewable sources, it's been outsourcing its pollution by building polluting coal-fired power plants all over the world, in East Europe, in the Balkans, in Africa, in Asia, and in Latin America.

Another example of China's deception concerns ozone. The ozone layer protects life on Earth from the sun's harmful ultraviolet radiation. Chemicals, specifically CFC-11, which created a giant hole in the ozone layer and caused an alarm among environmentalists, were banned under an international protocol that China also signed. However, the Chinese, true to their usual deception, were found, according to the journal Nature, to be illegally producing massive amounts of CFC-11 to use for insulation in their home construction industry. They have done so purely for financial benefits, even to the detriment of our planet and life on it.

China's water pollution is just as bad. China's seas, mangroves, wetlands, rivers, lakes, and groundwater are heavily polluted. Green algae sometimes erupt and cover huge swaths of beaches and lakes. Seas and rivers are

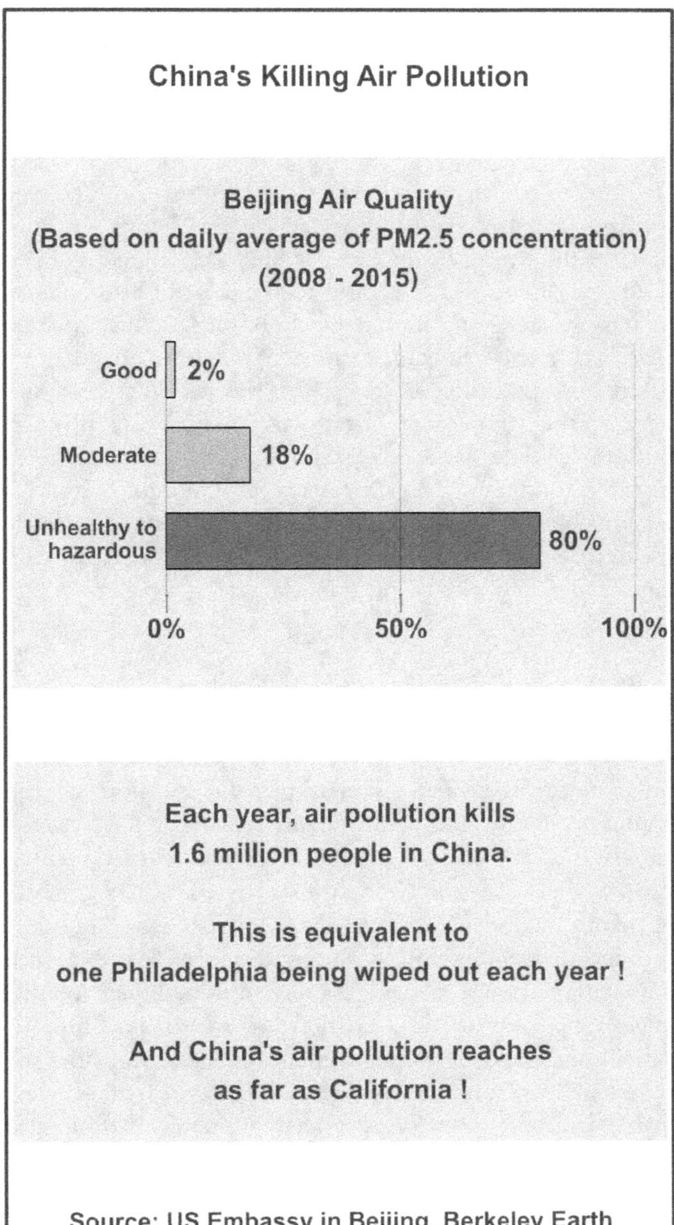
China's Killing Air Pollution

Beijing Air Quality
(Based on daily average of PM2.5 concentration)
(2008 - 2015)

Good 2%
Moderate 18%
Unhealthy to hazardous 80%

0% 50% 100%

Each year, air pollution kills
1.6 million people in China.

This is equivalent to
one Philadelphia being wiped out each year !

And China's air pollution reaches
as far as California !

Source: US Embassy in Beijing, Berkeley Earth

depleted of fish. Groundwater is contaminated to the point of being hazardous to health. And even rivers that are used for the drinking water supply can sometimes be filled with huge numbers of floating animal carcasses like pigs.

And China is exporting its destructive habits to other parts of the world. In the South China Sea, China has been destroying huge reefs in order to build artificial islands as military bases. In the Paracel Islands, which China snatched from Vietnam, hordes of Chinese tourists are destroying the pristine reefs. In the world's seas and oceans, the Chinese are destroying marine life through bottom-trawling and overfishing. And according to research done at the University of Georgia, China is responsible for more than a quarter of the world's plastic waste that finds its way into the oceans. This plastic waste kills turtles and birds, and contaminates the seafood that we eat.

China is also seriously jeopardizing the water resources of its neighboring countries. Countries in South and Southeast Asia whose very survival depends on rivers that originate in the high Tibetan plateau are now at the complete mercy of China, and have already started suffering from China's irresponsible upstream damming and water diversions on those rivers. The Chinese upstream activities affect the downstream countries through water pollution, unpredictable water levels, devastating floods, ravaging droughts, impediment of fish migration, loss of fish, erosion of riverbanks, loss of agricultural land, loss of human habitat, and loss of sediment. And China's irresponsible behavior reaches new highs. Indeed, China doesn't share valuable hydrological data with downstream countries, explaining that such data is an internal and security matter.

China's Stranglehold on Asian Rivers

China

Tibet

India

Indian
Ocean

1 Yellow River ——→ China

2 Yangtze ——→ China

3 Mekong ——→ China, Myanmar, Laos, Thailand, Cambodia, Vietnam

4 Salween ——→ China, Myanmar, Thailand

5 Irrawaddy ——→ China, Myanmar

6 Yarlung Tsangpo (Brahmaputra) ——→ China, India, Bangladesh

7 Ganges ——→ China, India, Bangladesh

8 Indus ——→ China, India, Pakistan

Nowhere are these Chinese nefarious activities more salient than in the Mekong river, which originates in China and then runs through the Southeast Asian countries of Laos, Myanmar, Thailand, Cambodia and Vietnam. These countries have been heavily affected by China's upstream activities. Not only have the agriculture and fishing industries of these countries been detrimentally affected, but the livelihoods of their people are at stake. According to reports such as those by International Rivers, China now has ten dams on the upper Mekong and plans to build many more. And not only has China been damming the upper Mekong like crazy, it's also been forcing the weak downstream countries to build questionable dams on their own soil, dams that usually benefit China more than they benefit the locals. China is also changing the Mekong's topography to facilitate trade by widening and dredging the river. This project has entailed ruining scenic wild areas, wiping rapids off the map, and blasting islets. China has used its strategic geographical position and economic clout to bring the downstream Southeast Asian countries to heel.

China is also contemplating another massive water diversion project that will adversely affect India and may lead to war between the two nuclear countries. Indeed, China is planning the diversion of the Yarlung Tsangpo in Tibet to the Taklimakan Desert in Xinjiang through a monumental thousand-kilometer tunnel. China is already building a six-hundred-kilometer tunnel in Yunnan as a prelude to its Tibetan project. This gargantuan project to turn the Taklimakan Desert into what the Chinese call a "California" will seriously affect the Brahmaputra river in northern India and may trigger a war between the two Asian giants.

Besides air and water pollution, the Chinese have also heavily polluted their soil. China's soil has a huge contamination problem. A 2014 government survey revealed that about 15% of all soil and about 20% of farmland was contaminated by all types of chemical pollutants from smelting plants, toxic fertilizers, toxic pesticides, toxic waste, and sewage irrigation. The contaminated farms have toxic soil that grows poisoned crops, such as rice laced with cadmium, a heavy metal that can accumulate in the kidneys and cause disease and even cancer. Such toxic soil is very expensive to clean up, and toxins can remain in the soil for centuries. Some villages in China have come to be called "Cancer Villages" because so many inhabitants there developed and died from cancer.

China threatening the world's wildlife

The Chinese are by far the world's biggest consumers of illegally poached wildlife and wildlife products. The Chinese have been greatly harming nature by driving many animals to near extinction. Indeed, as the Chinese have become prosperous, their disgusting eating habits, bogus medicinal concoctions, weird artifacts, and propensity to show off have led to the slaughter of unimaginable numbers of animals around the world, putting many of them in a vulnerable or extremely endangered status. The list of Chinese perverted needs includes the tusks of elephants, the horns of rhinos, the scales of pangolins, the casques of hornbills, the maws or swim bladders of the fish totoaba, all the body parts of tigers including their penises, the bile and paws of bears, the fins of sharks, the shells and flippers of turtles, and the list goes on.

In the case of elephants, the International Union for Conservation of Nature says that ivory poaching, which mainly feeds the perverted needs of East Asians and especially the Chinese, caused the deaths of more than 100,000 elephants in Africa over the last decade. That's a

The Chinese Threat to All Living Things

The Chinese have proven to be
a threat to every living thing
that they come in contact with.

Case in point is their treatment of animals,
which they mindlessly and cruelly
eat, maim, mistreat,
and drive to extinction.

Animal	What the Chinese harm it for
Elephant	Ivory
Rhino	Horn
Tiger	Bones, penis, eyes, brain, whiskers, tail, meat
Bear	Bile, gallbladder, paws
Donkey	Meat, skin
Dog	Meat
Cat	Meat
Civet cat	Meat
Pangolin	Scales
Whale	Entertainment
Wolf	Entertainment
Shark	Fins

whopping 20% of the elephant population!

Some of the beliefs that the Chinese cite when justifying their killings of wildlife are more superstitious than scientific. Thus, turtles, which can live for a long time, are thought to add to longevity and even cure cancer. Owls, which have good night vision, are thought to improve eyesight. Pangolins, which have scaly skins, are prescribed for skin diseases. And snake blood, for one reason or another, is thought to be an aphrodisiac.

In the case of shark fins, which are used to make a very expensive soup, scientific analysis has shown that the fins don't have any extraordinary ingredients, and are actually less nutritious than the shark meat that's discarded. The Chinese partake in such wasteful gastronomy just to showcase their wealth and satiate their vanity. Just to satisfy this Chinese craving, about seventy million sharks are killed for their fins each year according to estimates by the journal Marine Policy.

In the case of rhino horns, the Chinese and other East Asians are the reason for the poaching of rhinos because these people believe that the horn, shaped like a big erect phallus, can enhance their sex lives. However, scientists have shown that the horns are made of keratin, the protein that also makes our hair and nails, and don't have any medicinal benefits. Killing these beautiful majestic animals to the point of extinction is a crime against humanity. It serves these East Asian savages right that nature saddled them with puny penises!

China's "wildlife conservation" law allows the captive breeding of wild animals, such as bears and tigers, for commercial purposes, endorses the use of wildlife in traditional Chinese medicine and food for profit, and supports the use of wild animals for public entertainment.

The Chinese keep such animals in horrendous conditions, and treat them in unimaginably cruel ways. For example, in Chinese farms where bears are raised for Chinese medicine, the bile is extracted from living bears by inserting steel tubes into their bodies.

Killing our planet's living creatures on such a huge and reckless scale just to satisfy their weird palates, superstitious beliefs, and despicable egos is a crime against nature and humanity. The Chinese are truly a threat to our planet. Wherever the Chinese or Chinese companies go, whether it be Africa or South America or any other place, the indigenous wildlife suffers. For example, in South America, the Chinese there were responsible for the Jaguars being killed just for their fangs.

Sometimes one gets the feeling that the Chinese are some kind of aliens from another world, and nature is fighting against them. Indeed, one of their deviant eating habits, namely that of eating civet cats, caused the terrifying world epidemic of SARS, which killed thousands in China and caused deaths in 37 countries, according to the World Health Organization. One can't have sympathy or mercy for such unimaginably cruel and hopelessly uncivilized hordes that just keep multiplying, spreading, and destroying our poor planet like parasites.

4

IDEOLOGY

The Communist Party of China (CPC) has been in power since 1949 when it founded the People's Republic of China (PRC). This communist government is a totalitarian regime that exercises strict and absolute control over the country, and forbids any dissent or opposition. China has come to be synonymous with the CPC, and the Chinese government's policies reflect the CPC ideology.

Central to China's communist leaders' thinking is the absolute control of the whole population. Using an internal security apparatus with a budget that surpasses even that of national defense and a totally controlled media, the CPC has succeeded in not only consolidating its power but also in shaping the masses into a dangerously brainwashed and jingoistic populace that sings the praises of the CPC and marches to its propaganda drumbeat.

And now that China has developed into a powerful country, the CPC's agenda has expanded from a national scope to the international arena, where it's vying to expand its influence at the expense of the West.

China's schizophrenic communists

China's leaders have been facing a huge predicament in defining whom they, and the country, really are. In the first four decades of the PRC history, there was the Soviet Union to identify with and even emulate. It was simple back then for the PRC to identify itself as a communist country, and follow the Leninist-Marxist dogma. But then the Soviet Union collapsed in the last decade of the previous century, and the beacon of communism vanished. The dissolution of the Soviet Union left the PRC to fend for itself on the ideological front, and the result has been a China with contradictory principles and realities. Indeed, while the CPC has continued referring to itself and the country as being communist, or socialist with Chinese characteristics, the reality is that China has embraced ideas that are anathema to communism, ideas such as "to get rich is glorious."

Ever since Deng Xiaoping's assumption of power, China has had this predicament of defining its true ideological course. The great modernization drive since Deng's tenure has been a period during which the ideology, no matter how periodically reinforced, has taken a back seat to an economic development that reeks more of capitalism than communism or socialism. During this modernization drive, the CPC found itself lagging behind the pace of change that radically transformed China, and had to adopt a more pragmatic ideology that suited the facts on the ground.

This policy of the communists espousing capitalism while still hypocritically identifying themselves as communists has led to widespread corruption, including corruption of the minds. This corruption has pervaded not only the communist cadres but also the general population.

Truly, hypocrisy and deceit have come to mean the way of life in China.

Fortunately for China, its latest paramount leader, Xi Jinping, has come to realize that this situation was untenable and the CPC was running the risk of losing legitimacy and power. Xi, whose mantra is the dream of China's rejuvenation, has sought to drain the swamp, so to speak. Thus, he has called for a return to China's roots, not only the roots of the PRC and Mao's Thought, but also the roots of the Chinese civilization and Confucianism.

How the CPC will evolve is a big question. Deng once famously said that the CPC should "seek truth from facts." If such is the case, then the CPC may one day be correctly referred to as the Corrupt Party of China or Capitalist Party of China. No matter what slogans or tricks the CPC uses in the future to define itself, one thing for certain is that it's communist only in name.

China indoctrinating its masses

The way that the CPC has been able to maintain its absolute control of the country for so long has been through the implementation of a repressive police state with draconian laws, and more importantly through a propaganda machine that has totally brainwashed the populace into unquestioning conformity and subservience.

The communist propaganda and indoctrination starts from an early age in primary school as the Chinese are taught to follow the CPC line and cherish the communist leaders. Every school, up to and including the universities, has a CPC office. This office is the most important entity in the school and sets the overall policy for the school! Teachers, professors, principals and deans owe their jobs to the CPC and act as its enforcement agents on campuses.

In college, all students must take compulsory classes in communism and Marxism. In these politics classes, they also learn about the ideologies of their paramount leaders, such as Mao Zedong's *Thought*, Deng Xiaoping's *Theory*, Jiang Zemin's *Three Represents*, Hu Jintao's *Theory of Scientific Development*, and Xi's *Four Comprehensives*. Also, all freshmen, boys and girls, in high school and college must take a one-month military training course to learn about discipline, get some firearms experience, and develop loyalty to the CPC.

And Chinese leaders think that this type of school indoctrination is normal and must not only be continued but also reinforced. Thus, in 2016, president Xi said that universities must become ideological strongholds of the communist party and promote socialism with Chinese characteristics.

Not only are the schools strictly controlled by the CPC, but also so is the workplace. China's state enterprises have CPC committees that make sure that the party line is followed. In 2017, the CPC even came up with new criteria to evaluate the CEOs of these enterprises, criteria based on how well the CEOs upheld and promoted the party line in their companies.

And outside of schools and the workplace, the CPC propaganda is everywhere on TV, on the radio, in newspapers, in magazines, on posters, on billboards, and even on walls covered with slogans. The Chinese media strictly follows the CPC guidelines. No wonder that during a tour of media outlets in 2016, president Xi called on the media's absolute loyalty to the communist party, and asked the media to "bear the surname of the party," and to "love the party, protect the party."

Chinese Leaders' Evolving Theories

Leader	Theory Name	Meaning
Mao Zedong	Thought	Marxism-Leninism with Chinese characteristics
Deng Xiaoping	Theory	Socialism with Chinese characteristics
Jiang Zemin	Three Represents	CPC leads in social, economic, and political reform
Hu Jintao	Theory of Scientific Development	Harmonious social and economic development
Xi Jinping	Four Comprehensives	Prosperity, reform, rule of law, and party discipline

The media is so controlled that even the delivery of news is strictly choreographed. Thus, news on TV, on the radio, and in newspapers has to follow the political-hierarchy order, and must report first on the paramount leader, second on the prime minister, and third on other members of the Politburo. Such a contrived and structured orchestration of the news can be seen daily on TV during the national news programs when anchormen read the news like robots programmed to regurgitate well-scripted monologues.

China's news anchors really look and sound like lifeless brainless blockheads that just read and recite carefully scripted news. In fact, Xinhua, China's news agency, announced in 2018 the creation of AI anchors that look and sound like its real anchors. These AI anchors will be the perfect propaganda tools for the CPC to keep brainwashing and controlling the populace, as they will be used to deliver the news nonstop, 24/7 all year round.

Besides the traditional media, the Internet is also strictly controlled by the CPC. The Chinese government has built what's been referred to as the *Great Firewall* and trained a huge army of programmers and hackers for the purpose of sanitizing the Internet out of any information that's deemed unacceptable. For example, the Chinese name for *Winnie the Pooh* and pictures of that cuddly bear are blocked on Chinese social media because some bloggers compared it to president Xi.

Anytime the Chinese censors don't like some news coverage from abroad, it's blocked. Sometimes not only web pages are blocked but also whole websites become inaccessible. Some of the websites that are either totally blocked, frequently blocked or slowed down include social media such as Facebook and Twitter, search media such as Google and its various services, reference media such as

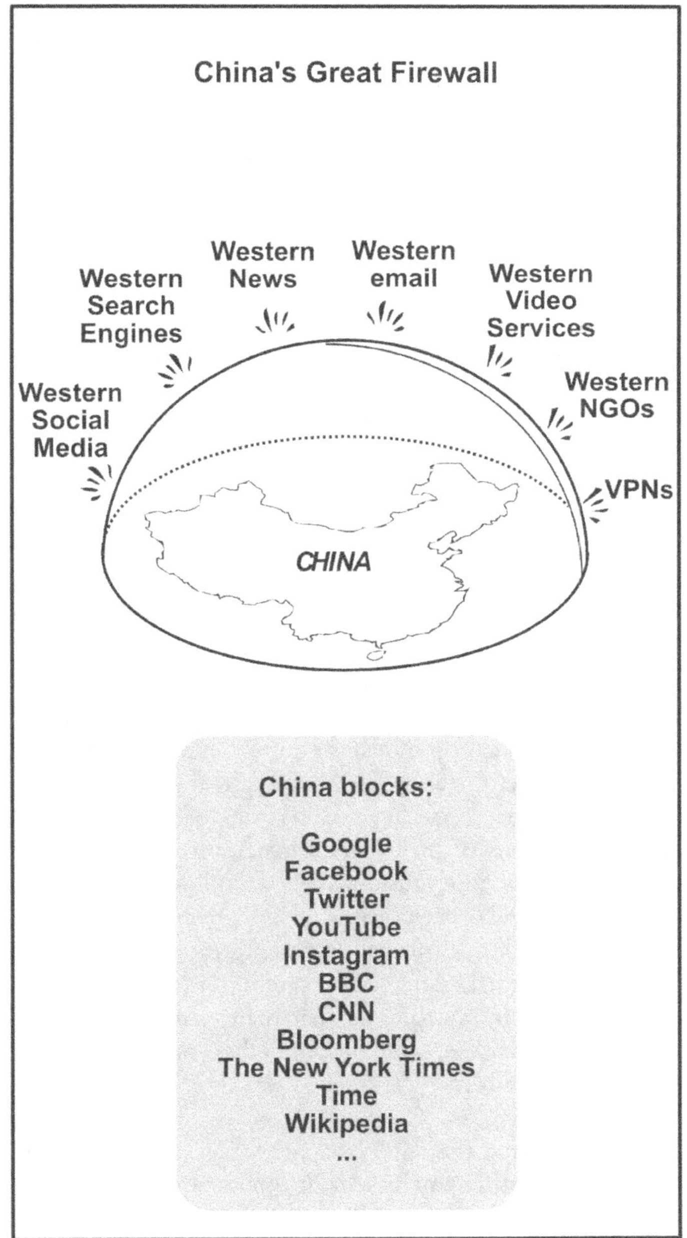
China's Great Firewall
Western Search Engines
Western News
Western email
Western Video Services
Western Social Media
Western NGOs
VPNs
CHINA
China blocks:
Google
Facebook
Twitter
YouTube
Instagram
BBC
CNN
Bloomberg
The New York Times
Time
Wikipedia
...

Wikipedia, and news media such as CNN, BBC, and VOA.

Some Chinese try to circumvent the *Great Firewall* by using VPNs (Virtual Private Networks). However, the government of Xi Jinping has cracked down hard on these lifelines to the outside world. For example, Apple was forced by China to remove many apps offering VPN services that could be used to bypass the *Great Firewall*.

And the Chinese government isn't just censoring the Internet. It uses the Internet as a formidable propaganda tool. For example, the Chinese government uses and pays a legion of social media commentators, the so-called "50 Cent Party," to post messages supporting the government policies.

The CPC's pervasive, invasive, exclusive and unrelenting propaganda and indoctrination of the masses has been without a doubt a great success because the result is that the great majority of the Chinese toe the party line. And the CPC is constantly honing its methods, such as when dealing with the young generation of Chinese. Thus, in 2017, the education minister said universities must make ideology classes "trendy" in order to appeal to young minds. Also the recording studios run by the CPC have released all types of propaganda material to appeal to the young, such as rap music videos extolling China while bashing the West, cartoons showing president Xi's fight against corruption, cartoons promoting the Politburo, and videos about president Xi's catchphrase, the "China Dream." One funny thing is that many such releases are recorded in English, with accents that range from the native to the weird!

One card that the CPC constantly plays to consolidate its power and stifle any dissent or opposition is that of the "threat" from the outside, be it the West, Japan or other countries. China's anti-Western and anti-Japanese communist propaganda has totally brainwashed and radicalized its citizenry. This jingoistic stratagem has over the years led to a radical change in the Chinese mindset. The great majority of today's Chinese have been molded into jingoistic and truculent xenophobes, who are not only very suspicious of but also overtly hostile toward foreigners, especially Westerners. The CPC can at any time and instantly whip up nationalist fervor and mobilize mobs of these nationalists against a foreign target. For example, Americans and American companies, such as McDonald's and KFC, can suddenly find themselves the subject of harassment and demonstrations for the slightest US provocation.

The CPC's propaganda campaign has been so successful that there's hardly any significant opposition to the government. One example of how effective the campaign has been is that nowadays not only the government says that the Dalai Lama is evil, but actually most Chinese would also say so. Diversity of opinion seems to be anathema to the communist dogma.

Finally, while the CPC's propaganda has been very effective, the propaganda against foreigners sometimes reaches ridiculous levels. For example, Chinese patriotic movies always portray the Japanese soldiers as inferior adversaries that the Chinese whip at will in every encounter. Somehow the fact that the Japanese had superior armed forces and occupied parts of China for years is always overlooked. Another example is that even in institutions of higher learning, intimate contact with foreigners is discouraged or frowned upon. Thus, officials in Beijing Language (and Culture) University, perhaps China's leading institution for teaching Chinese to foreigners, have for years held regular seminars for the Chinese students there to remind them of not developing intimate relationships with foreigners. Also, in 2017, a national campaign was launched to warn students of all ages against foreign spies. Pamphlets, posters, and animations were distributed across schools nationwide. One particular piece of this campaign, called "Dangerous Love," warned students against falling for the sweet talk of foreigners because they could be spies.

China's institutionalized lies

The CPC has not only been hypocritical about its own identity, it has also come up with a set of institutionalized lies to feed the population and the rest of the world. The Chinese leaders think that just by labeling something with the tag "with Chinese Characteristics," they can make it kosher! Today's Chinese, led by the example of their leaders, are living and participating in an ethos of deception.

The foremost deception is that when it comes to the system of government in China, the CPC says that it's "Socialism with Chinese characteristics." Such a characterization is complete baloney because the fact is that there's a very rich, privileged, and corrupt elite while the great masses toil and struggle for a living. The gap between the rich and poor in China has reached alarming levels.

Another deception is that of "Governance with Chinese characteristics." Thus, when it comes to governance, the CPC says that China is a people's republic. What's actually true is that the people have no say. The CPC governs with an iron hand and epitomizes corrupt governance without any transparency.

The next deception is that of "Democracy with

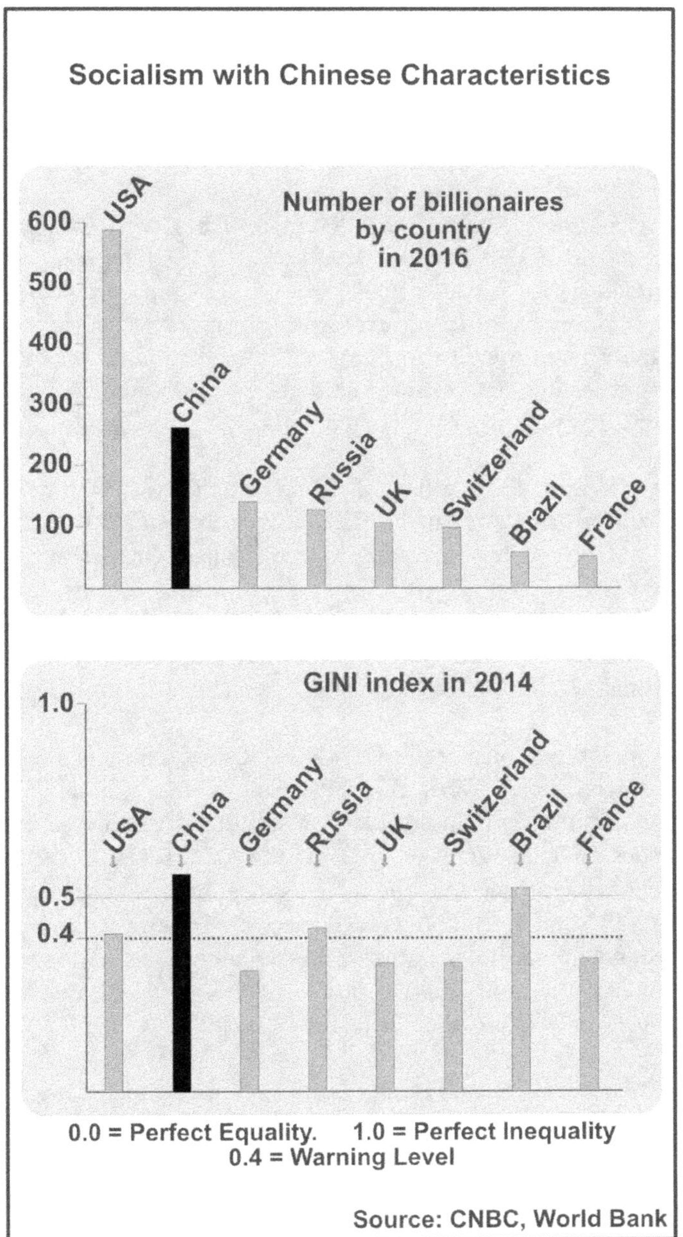
Socialism with Chinese Characteristics
Number of billionaires
by country
in 2016
600
500
400
300
200
100
USA
China
Germany
Russia
UK
Switzerland
Brazil
France
GINI index in 2014
1.0
0.5
0.4
USA
China
Germany
Russia
UK
Switzerland
Brazil
France
0.0 = Perfect Equality.   1.0 = Perfect Inequality
0.4 = Warning Level
Source: CNBC, World Bank

Chinese characteristics." What the CPC says is that China promotes its people's rights and is a democracy. What's actually true is that China is an authoritarian autocracy or oligarchy where the paramount leader and Politburo exercise complete and absolute control.

Another lie is that of "Human rights with Chinese characteristics." What the CPC says is that China respects human rights. What's actually true is that China persecutes any opponents of its government, oppresses its minorities, exploits its migrant population, exploits Third World countries in a new form of colonialism, and vetoes human rights resolutions at the United Nations.

Another lie is that of "Free media with Chinese characteristics." What the CPC says is that China's media is as free and objective as Western media. What's actually true is that China's media is strictly controlled, censored, and used as a government propaganda machine. According to the 2017 World Press Freedom Index, China ranks a dismal 176 out of 180 countries.

Another blatant lie is "Pacifism with Chinese characteristics." What the CPC says is that China is a pacifist country focused solely on self-defense and regional issues. What's actually true is that China is a rising militaristic power that's bullying its neighbors, and building aircraft carriers and overseas bases to project its power around the world. Taiwan's government said it best when in 2019 it said that China's claim of its "peaceful development" was the "lie of the century."

Another ridiculous lie is "Economy with Chinese characteristics." The CPC says that China has a market economy, and engages in fair trade as a member of the WTO. What's actually true is that China actively engages in piracy, counterfeiting, dumping, illegal subsidies, currency manipulation, and stock market manipulation.

And another mockery of the truth is "Social harmony with Chinese characteristics." What the CPC says is that China is one big happy family where everyone is treated fairly and the same. What's actually true is that communist China resembles Imperial China in that an elite controls all the power and wealth. China is a country where the rich and poor live by different rules. Thus, rich and powerful families like that of present paramount leader, Xi Jinping, have amassed great wealth through corruption and get to keep their ill-gotten gains, while the poor keep toiling in misery and under tyranny.

Xi is presently leading a huge campaign against corruption, but he has ulterior motives, those of sidelining his opponents and consolidating his power. Indeed, while Xi is fighting corruption, his family and the families of friendly Red Princelings, offspring of CPC officials, like him are untouched. Xi's official annual salary is about $22,000, and was of course lower before in his other government jobs, and yet his family and extended family hold assets worth hundreds of millions of dollars! Rich Chinese, like Xi's family, have become quite savvy at hiding their wealth by spreading it among their extended families, registering it under the names of close business associates, and concealing it using offshore tax havens. Western media, such as Bloomberg and the New York Times, that reported on such corruption in China had their websites blocked in China, and their new visa requests denied. And Chinese activists who call for China's politicians to disclose their assets have been jailed for "disturbing the public order."

The fact is that most if not all rich Chinese got their wealth through corruption because that's how the People's Republic of China has always functioned, especially after

Deng assumed power. Any campaign against corruption in China should snare almost every rich Chinese. Thus, campaigns like the one currently led by Xi are targeted campaigns, that is they have ulterior motives than just to fight against corruption.

The CPC's claim that China is a harmonious society is total nonsense. The system protects the corrupt rich and powerful, while the rest of the population is treated like second-class citizens. Poor people and farmers around the country suffer injustices such as land dispossession and other unjust treatment, and are at the mercy of the local authorities and rich people. When these victims try to take their grievances to Beijing, thugs employed by the local authorities try to prevent them from ever reaching their destination, and in case they do make it to Beijing, they are hassled there too. The Chinese are known for their utter cruelty toward the helpless and the weak. One example of how the rich and poor live by different rules in China is that when the spoiled kids of rich and powerful families commit reckless crimes, such as running down some poor pedestrians while engaging in reckless street car races, those families make sure that their kids never spend any time in prison by hiring or forcing some poor body doubles to do the time instead.

Such institutionalized and blatant corruption of the truth has no limit. And this zeitgeist of lies and deceit carries on to foreign affairs and dealings. For example, just a few years ago, when foreigners started talking about China's rise as a new power, the Chinese were incensed. The Chinese leaders, media and pundits all vehemently denied it! Even though all the economic and military statistics were there to prove such a rise, the Chinese still denied it and strongly objected to Westerners using the word *rise*! Only recently have the Chinese come clean and admitted such a fact. Another example of blatant lying is about espionage. When the US published a report about Chinese espionage in the US, guess what! China vehemently denied spying. This really takes the cake: what country doesn't spy? All countries do. Another example is that in 2017 when China said it wasn't retaliating against South Korea for deploying the US anti-missile defense system THAAD, a deployment which by the way was needed against a belligerent and dangerous North Korea, China was blatantly lying because the facts were out there for anyone to see. Indeed, China did punish South Korea by cancelling Chinese tours to that country, by cancelling tours by South Korean music bands, and by closing stores that belonged to Lotte, a South Korean company. And another example is that of the Spratly Islands in the South China Sea. In 2015, president Xi promised that they would not be militarized. However, soon afterwards, satellite imagery showed that China was heavily militarizing them.

China's international propaganda

China's international propaganda has gone into overdrive during the reign of the current Chinese paramount leader, Xi. Xi has exhorted the Chinese media to go out to the rest of the world and tell the China story, i.e. praise the CPC and discredit the West. Using its economic muscle and taking advantage of the West's openness, China has mounted a formidable international propaganda campaign. China is now using this soft power to spread its influence around the world.

In radio, state-run China Radio International (CRI) broadcasts around the world in more than 60 languages via shortwave, the Internet and other media. In addition, according to Reuters, CRI has control over a network of radio stations around the world, including America, and uses this network to broadcast China-friendly programming. CRI hides its control of these overseas stations by using subsidiaries and front companies.

In TV, China's main TV organization, CCTV, launched in 2017 a global media organization called CGTN that delivers China-friendly news in English, Spanish, French, Arabic and Russian. CGTN content is delivered via various digital platforms including cable and the Internet.

In the print media, China publishes English papers, such as China Daily and Global Times. The Chinese also place favorable articles and advertisements in foreign media.

On the Internet, China is using not only its own websites for propaganda, but also those of the West. Thus, even though Facebook is blocked in China, some Chinese media like CCTV and People's Daily have Facebook pages. These Chinese organizations fill their Facebook pages with English-language posts and seem to have huge numbers of Likes. However, some investigative reporting by Quartz Media has shown that these Likes are mostly fake and come from Third World countries where it's very easy to buy Likes through click-farms.

In movies, China is using Hollywood to portray a positive image of itself. China uses the huge size of its market, it's the world's second largest movie box office, to force Hollywood to modify its movie scripts to China's liking. Thus, for Hollywood movies to be screened in China, their plots must not depict China in any negative way. Hollywood has already been conditioned to such self-censure, and studios have become a sort of propaganda tool for the CPC. Another way that China is influencing Hollywood is that the Chinese have been buying Hollywood assets, such as movie studios, and investing in Hollywood movies.

And in education, China is using its Confucius Institutes to further its influence and promote its ideology around the world. Though China officially claims that Confucius Institutes are set up by its Ministry of Education, the truth is that they are created by the United Front Work Department, a CPC organization responsible for guiding overseas influence and propaganda activities.

Confucius Institutes use the attractiveness of learning the Chinese language to influence Americans of all ages as they offer courses to middle-schoolers, high-schoolers, university students, and members of the community. These institutes provide not just education in the Chinese language but also come with an army of Chinese teachers who are brainwashed hardcore nationalists. Hundreds of such institutes have sprouted around the world, including dozens in American schools, all with the objective of projecting China's soft power.

Confucius Institutes are under the control of the CPC and serve its agenda. They try to present a sanitized image of China that appeals to the rest of the world, especially the West. Thus, any discussion of thorny questions like Tibet, Xinjiang, Taiwan and Tiananmen is taboo in these institutes. The true nature of the Confucius Institutes was revealed by a quote from a former senior leader of the CPC, Li Changchun, who said, "The Confucius brand has a natural attractiveness. Using the excuse of teaching Chinese language, everything looks reasonable and logical."

Confucius Institutes go even further in stifling the freedom of expression on US and world campuses because they promote the authoritarian and repressive policies of the CPC. For example, an American university was forced to cancel a visit by the Dalai Lama because of strong

China's Soft Power Swamping the US

110 Confucius Institutes,
under the control of the CPC,
have spread across the US,
and the number keeps growing.
The institutes branch out to even more hubs
called Confucius Classrooms.

AL 3	HI 1	MA 3	NM 1	SD 1
AK 1	ID 2	MI 4	NY 10	TN 3
AZ 2	IL 2	MN 2	NC 2	TX 6
AR 1	IN 3	MS	ND 1	UT 3
CA 7	IA 1	MO 2	OH 4	VT
CO 2	KS 2	MT 1	OK 1	VA 3
CT 1	KY 2	NE 1	OR 2	WA 1
DE 1	LA 2	NV 1	PA 2	WV 1
FL 6	ME 1	NH 1	RI 2	WI 1
GA 6	MD 1	NJ 2	SC 2	WY

Source: Hanban

objections from its Confucius Institute. Confucius Institutes are also suspected of engaging in espionage and the surveillance of Chinese students abroad. And Senator Rubio of Florida stated in 2018 that "There is mounting concern about the Chinese government's increasingly aggressive attempts to use 'Confucius Institutes' and other means to influence foreign academic institutions and critical analysis of China's past history and present policies."

Also in education, the CPC uses the overseas Chinese students' associations to further its agenda. These associations are known to be very nationalistic, and to have close links with and follow orders from Chinese consulates and embassies.

One example of the nefarious activities of these student associations is the attempt by one of them at the University of California San Diego to force that university to rescind an invitation to the Dalai Lama to give a graduation speech. The excuse given by the association, and one commonly used by the CPC to demonize things it doesn't approve of, was that the invitation "hurt the feelings of the Chinese people." Another example is that when a Chinese student in the US spoke of how she loved the fresh air in the US, other Chinese students in the US vilified her for "criticizing her country" and she got crucified by the Chinese media. She received all sorts of threats, and had to issue and apology and beg for forgiveness.

An eye-opening development in recent years is that some Chinese Americans, such as congressmen, and Chinese-American associations defend the mainland Chinese and criticize American officials, such as the FBI Director, for voicing concerns about China's influence in the US. These Chinese Americans now feel emboldened to

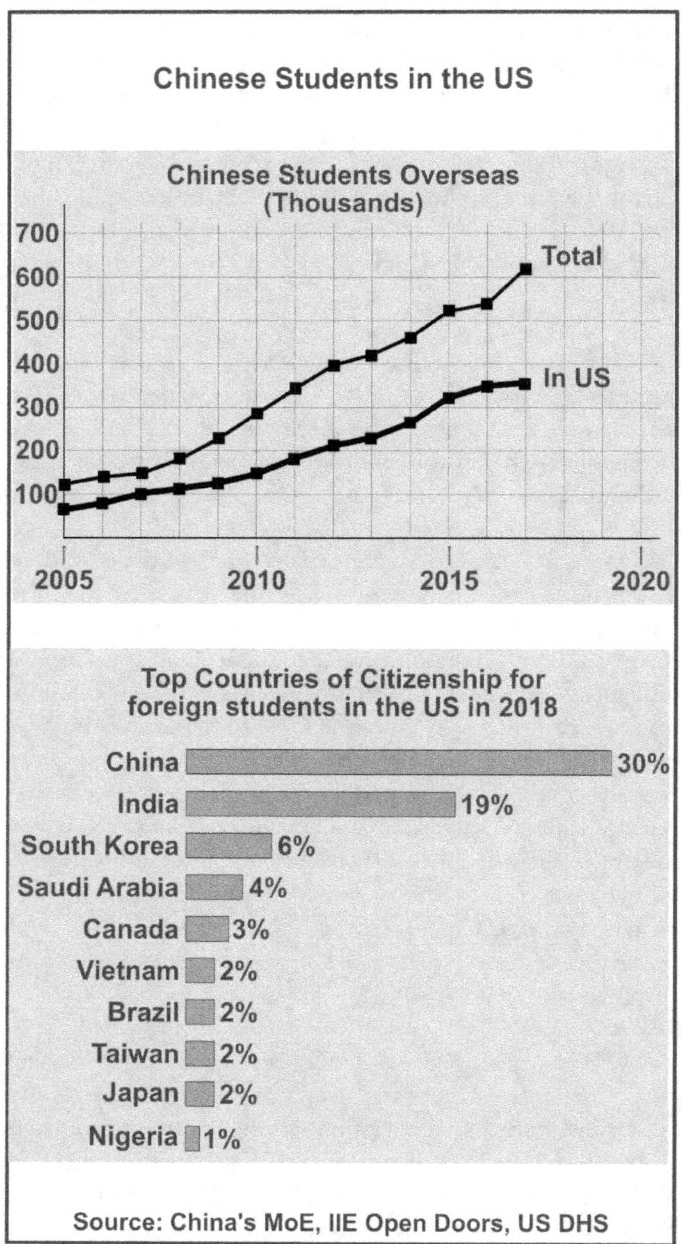

Chinese Students in the US

Chinese Students Overseas
(Thousands)

700
600
500
400
300
200
100

Total
In US

2005
2010
2015
2020

Top Countries of Citizenship for
foreign students in the US in 2018

China 30%
India 19%
South Korea 6%
Saudi Arabia 4%
Canada 3%
Vietnam 2%
Brazil 2%
Taiwan 2%
Japan 2%
Nigeria 1%

Source: China's MoE, IIE Open Doors, US DHS

support China against the US. In February 2018, when the FBI Director Christopher Wray testified at a congressional hearing that Chinese students and scholars posed a national security threat to the US, Chinese-American members of Congress from California and New York jumped to the defense of China. One of these Chinese-American congressmen stated, "I condemn these remarks entirely and reject these dangerous attempts to build a case that Chinese students, professors and scholars should be viewed with more suspicion than others." This is a very dangerous development. Maybe Chinese Americans should do well to remember the case of Jerry Chun Shing Lee, a naturalized US citizen from China who worked for the CIA for more than a decade, and who was arrested in 2018 as a suspect for helping China to uncover, kill and jail some 20 CIA informants in China. His case crippled the CIA operations in China.

Another sickening example of the CPC's international propaganda in the education field was the Chinese government conning of many naïve foreign students in China into appearing in moronic videos to sing the praises of the Chinese paramount leader Xi. In those videos, the foreign students are heard lavishing love and admiration on the Chinese strongman. The whole setup stinks and reminds one of Uganda's once dictator Idi Amin Dada.

And one final tool in China's soft-power arsenal is taking advantage of the West's openness, venality, and political dysfunction. For example, China was able to display a video supporting its claim to the whole of the South China Sea on a gigantic screen in Times Square in New York City for many days. The US could only dream of such access in Tiananmen Square. Another example is China using lobbying groups of moneygrubbing American lawyers, politicians and well-connected people who wouldn't think twice of selling out and betraying their country for a small fortune. And another example is that China can point to the deplorable state of many Western democracies that have become the laughingstock of international opinion.

The CPC's ideological campaign has allowed it to consolidate its power and totally turn the Chinese populace into an army of jingoistic zombies that march to its ideological beat. Now the CPC's push has turned to swaying the international opinion and winning the ideological war against the West. The frightening thing is that China is gradually winning this global ideological war.

5

POLITICS

China is a one-party state where the Communist Party of China (CPC) has ruled unchallenged since 1949. The CPC controls all the organs of power, including the executive branch made of the State Council, the legislative branch made of the National People's Congress, the judiciary from the lowest municipal courts to the highest court, the Central Military Commission, the armed forces, the police, and the militia. The CPC also controls the media, the schools, the biggest enterprises, the banks, and basically everything else in the Chinese society, down to the neighborhood committees. With such a pervasive presence and an authoritarian regime, the CPC has been able to maintain a firm control of the country and suppress any domestic dissent or opposition.

And on the international scene, China has long ago shed its Third World non-aligned policy, and turned into a rising belligerent power with its own policies and core interests. Both domestically and internationally, the CPC has been pursuing Mao Zedong philosophy of "Political power grows out of the barrel of a gun."

China's "democratic" dictatorship

It may come as a surprise to many, but China considers itself a democracy! However, China's definition of democracy is different from that of the West. The Chinese variation of democracy as promulgated by Mao Zedong is that the state represents and acts on behalf of the people, but in order to guarantee that this is the case, the state must always be under the absolute control of the CPC. While this idea may have had some noble ideals behind it, it has one critical deficiency that has doomed communism around the world: absolute power absolutely corrupts. Without checks and balances as in Western democracies, power always leads to rampant corruption and the ultimate collapse of the system.

The problem with the communist leaders being the sole monitors of "democracy" in China is the classic case of who monitors the monitors. Indeed, with the CPC holding absolute power, corruption and abuse of power have become so rampant as to define the ethos of the modern Chinese society. The CPC has been able to hold on to power only through the implementation of a repressive police state.

In any case, the Chinese government is always proud to remind foreigners that China has eight parties in addition to the ruling CPC. Forget about the fact that the CPC totally controls the government and the other parties themselves! To the Chinese government this is still democracy. Well, democracy with Chinese characteristics of course. Maybe an appropriate name for it should be *"Democrazy."*

The other Chinese parties are some types of remnants from the time of the founding of the Republic of China,

China's Democratic Dictatorship

China is a self-declared democracy,

but

only the CPC can rule !

List of officially recognized parties in China

Party	Membership
CPC	80,000,000
RCCK	65,000
CDL	156,000
CDNCA	85,000
CAPD	81,000
CPWDP	80,000
CZGP	20,000
JS	80,000
TDSL	1,800

Source: People's Daily

and their activities and membership are strictly controlled by the CPC. Their membership has not increased much since their establishment and numbers in the mere thousands compared to that of the CPC, which has tens of millions of dedicated members.

Thus, power in China rests with the CPC and its paramount leader. The paramount leader is of course always a Han male, and usually holds three important titles. The first title is that of General Secretary of the CPC. The second title is that of Chairman of the Central Military Commission (CMC). And the third title is that of President of China. Of these three titles, that of Chairman of the CMC is arguably the most important. This is the title that the paramount leader usually holds on to the longest while handing power to a successor to make sure that the transition in power goes smoothly. The current paramount leader, Xi Jinping, has enhanced this military title by also specifically designating himself as the commander-in-chief of China's armed forces.

Xi Jinping is by all accounts the strongest Chinese leader since Mao Zedong and Deng Xiaoping. After his accession to power in 2012, he quickly consolidated his power in the CPC, the armed forces, and the country as a whole. In the CPC, he weakened and marginalized other cliques and got rid of potential opponents. He engineered the dismissal and life imprisonment of his two most powerful rivals under the main charge of corruption, a charge that was very easy to prove since all CPC bigwigs are corrupt to the hilt. He consolidated his control of the CPC by controlling with his cronies the politburo, and the propaganda, anti-corruption and organization departments. He also got the CPC to designate him as the "core" of the party leadership, leaving no doubt as to who was in charge. In the armed forces, Xi brought the generals to heel by going all out against the senior officers, again using the

China's Paramount Leaders

MAO Zedong: The Great Helmsman

Failings:
- *Population explosion*
- *Starvation of millions*
- *Cultural Revolution*

DENG Xiaoping: The Great Modernist

Failings:
- *Tolerance of corruption*
- *Tiananmen Square massacre*

JIANG Zemin: The Caretaker

Failings:
- *Rampant corruption*
- *Undermining of his successor*

HU Jintao: The Red Dogmatist

Failings:
- *Inability to consolidate power*
- *Inability to reign in the military*
- *Lopsided wealth distribution*

XI Jinping: The Emperor

Failings:
- *Too much concentration of power*
- *Cultivation of a personality cult*
- *Suppression of any dissent*
- *Foreign hegemony*

Source: Zhang Zhenshi, www.kremlin.ru, Agencia Brasil

charge of corruption, a charge that again was easy to prove because of the rampant corruption in the senior ranks of the armed forces. Xi was fully cognizant of how those generals treated his predecessor with disrespect, and cut them down to size by engineering their dismissal or imprisonment. Xi also revamped the armed forces by downgrading the army, which used to be the center of power of all the armed forces, and by elevating friendly officers from the air force and navy. And under his rule, censorship, repression, and surveillance have intensified as he engineered the stifling of any dissent by ruthlessly persecuting and prosecuting rights activists, and by making the media even more of a propaganda machine. Thus, hundreds of human rights lawyers have recently been persecuted, detained, jailed, beaten, and stripped of their licenses to practice law by the authorities. In one case, a lawyer was told he couldn't practice law anymore because he opposed the CPC, and such behavior did not meet the standards required to practice law!

Xi also established a cult of personality, promoting his image as the country's benevolent father figure, and is omnipresent in posters everywhere. There's even a slick primetime TV game show about his life and his "Thought." The show is called *Studying Xi in the New Era*.

The failure to designate a successor to Xi at the 19th party congress in October 2017 and the abolition of presidential term limits at the National People's Congress (NPC) session in March 2018 only served to confirm that Xi has set himself up for an open-ended dictatorial rule. Xi has put all the power under him and his cronies. He has assumed the roles of President of China, General Secretary of the CPC, Chairman of the CMC, and Commander-in-chief of the armed forces. Also, besides being declared the *core* of the party leadership, he has made the CPC include his ideology, called *Xi Jinping Thought on Socialism with*

Chinese Characteristics for a New Era, or *Xi Jinping Thought* for short, into China's constitution. Centers dedicated to "studying" his thought have sprung throughout the country.

The paramount leader is helped in his rule of the CPC and the country by a small committee called the Politburo Standing Committee, or Politburo for short, a group that usually consist of five to nine members, including the paramount leader. The Politburo is the ultimate decision maker in China. The Chinese "parliament," called the National People's Congress, is just a rubber stamp. Whatever the paramount leader and Politburo want, that congress approves. And not only approve, but usually approve with overwhelming majorities of 99% or more. It seems that the number 99 is a fixture not only in the prices of goods but also in the approval ratings of dictatorships!

The Politburo members have historically represented different factions or cliques within the CPC. These cliques have been entrenched for decades of leadership and have continued their influence by promoting their members inside the communist party and the armed forces. The current strongman Xi Jinping has effectively put an end to that practice. Thus, Xi not only reduced the size of the Politburo but also filled it and the armed forces with his allies and protégés so as to safeguard his position and ensure his legacy.

China's totalitarian regime

The CPC is paranoid about any challenge to its rule, and uses all means necessary to prevent, control, and suppress it. Dissent is anathema to the communist Chinese leaders who use a variety of ways in order to maintain total control of the country.

First, the paramount leader and the Politburo wield all the power in China. Whatever they dictate to the CPC and the country becomes law. Other government entities, such as the National People's Congress and the Chinese People's Political Consultative Conference, are mere rubber stamps that always do and ratify what the CPC hierarchy demands.

Second, China has invested heavily in its security apparatus. It's an open secret that the budget for domestic security is greater than that of national defense! China uses its domestic security apparatus, which consists of the Ministry of Public Security, the Ministry of State Security, the police, the People's Armed Police, and the militias, to keep an ironhanded authoritarian control of the country. This security apparatus is aware of what's happening in every little corner of China. For example, neighborhoods are monitored by neighborhood watch committees that keep an eye on every little detail and immediately report any suspicious activities to the police. Besides the prying eyes of these neighborhood committees and the ubiquitous surveillance cameras, plainclothes police are also stationed everywhere and can spring to action at any moment. The security apparatus is complemented by the oppressive judiciary, which is totally subservient to the CPC and acts as its persecuting and prosecuting arm. In some instances, China even calls on its armed forces to suppress dissent, as it did in the Tiananmen Square Massacre.

Third, the CPC strictly controls the workplace, education, and the media. Thus, in every state-owned company and organization there's a CPC committee, which has the last say on any decisions. The same is true with education where all schools, including the universities, which are supposedly institutions of higher learning and open thinking, are led by CPC committees. And of course media in China is the mouthpiece of the CPC. Such omnipresence allows the CPC to control the people throughout their lives, from kindergarten to retirement and death.

Fourth, China engages in egregious repression of its people and abuse of its human rights. The CPC aggressively stifles any dissent and persecutes any activists or opponents. Any opposition to or demonstration against the government is immediately squashed and its leaders vilified, imprisoned, or even killed. Thus, there have been crackdowns on human-rights activists, lawyers for the poor and oppressed, and peaceful advocates for political reform. China's most famous artist Weiwei was persecuted and arrested on trumped up charges of "economic crimes" because he advocated some basic freedoms. The writer Liu Xiaobo, who called for political reform and who won the Nobel Peace Prize, was jailed in 2008 under the false charge of "inciting subversion of state power," and died in 2017 while still incarcerated. One ordinary guy who said the media belonged to the people and not the party was accused of trying to topple the government. And the Dalai Lama, another Nobel Peace Prize winner who defends the rights of his people in Tibet, is treated by the Chinese government as the evil agent of the West and isn't even allowed to return home.

Repression of opposition can be firm and thorough. For example, in 2011, when farmers in a Guangdong village rebelled against their communist leaders who kept unfairly dispossessing them of their farmland, the communist government sealed off the village from the outside world with barbed wire and censored any information from and about it. Another example is that anytime there's a major event in China, such as the Olympics or a visit by a prominent foreign dignitary, the government rounds up potential protestors and opposition figures and either locks them up or places them under house arrest. And another example is that China will go to any length to suppress opposition. Thus, some suspected opponents were kidnapped in Hong Kong and foreign countries, like Thailand, and brought back to China where they were coerced into making false confessions. Such confessions, made under duress because of blackmail and threats against families, are broadly broadcast on national TV in order to discredit the opponents. Such repressions indicate the true nature of communist China, a brutal police state where security forces not only actively harass dissidents but also engage in many reprehensible acts such as beatings, torture, and killings.

Fifth, the CPC preaches uniformity in all spheres, and sometimes goes to preposterous extremes to enforce it. Thus, even though China is geographically as big as the US and spans five international time zones, one more than the continental US, the Chinese government was so hell-bent on maintaining uniformity that it made China one single time zone. Thus, when it's 10am in Beijing, it's also 10am 3,000 miles west in the province of Xinjiang, although the sun may be just rising in Xinjiang! The natives of Xinjiang, mainly the Uighurs, don't adhere to this communist system of time keeping, and instead use their own local time, which is two hours behind. The CPC emphasis on uniformity is so extreme as to reach ridiculous proportions; indeed, top CPC leaders all strive to maintain the same demeanor when in public, and also the same appearance, not only in clothes but also in hairstyles! Such thinking is indicative of the CPC's paranoia about any kind of diversity, and propensity for strict control.

Sixth, the CPC employs the pretext of a constant threat from the outside world to keep and reinforce its grip on power. Thus, xenophobia and suspicion of foreigners is actively, if not always publicly, abetted, while the flames of

All of China is on Beijing Time !!

The communist party is so paranoid
about the breakup of the country
that it made the whole of China,
a country bigger than the US,
one single time zone !!

Standard Time Zones of the World

UTC + 5 | UTC + 6 | UTC + 7 | UTC + 8 | UTC + 9

UTC + 8

(UTC = GMT)

nationalism and jingoism are constantly fanned. The antagonism toward foreigners is sometimes carried to extremes. Thus, while employees in sensitive government posts understandably cannot have foreign spouses, the definition of sensitive is a bit ridiculous as it sometimes includes such mundane jobs as journalists.

Seventh, the government has turned to high tech to enhance its control of the population. China has deployed more surveillance equipment, such as cameras, throughout its territory than any other country. And now it's using that real-time data and other data collected online and otherwise to build a huge database that profiles each of its citizens. This database is truly comprehensive and includes biometric data, medical history, work data, financial transactions, and online activities. And what's even more incredible is that China is trying to leverage this huge amount of data to not only keep an eye on its people but also to try to predict their activities. Thus, the government's goal is to know each individual to the point of being able to predict his or her intentions or next move.

China's oppression of its minorities

Another way that the CPC maintains total control of the country is by keeping China's minorities, of which it's always suspicious, marginalized and under constant and strict control. Thus, the great majority, more than 90%, of the top government posts in China are reserved for the Han majority. This Han domination extends to all levels of government, from the national one to the provinces. In addition, the top leadership in any region always goes to a Han male. For example, in "autonomous" provinces the locals such as the Tibetans or Uighurs may be appointed as puppet governors, but the top provincial leaders, i.e. the general secretaries of the provincial communist parties, are always Han.

The fact is the Han not only mistrust their minorities but also look down on them. For example, the top Han official in the restive Xinjiang province once stereotyped the native Uighurs in his province by stating that "They're not concerned about terrorism but rather they're happy dancing." He basically referred to them as happy-go-lucky fools. And in Tibet, the Han look down on Tibetans for being dark-skinned and consider them as being inferior.

Among China's minorities' regions, Xinjiang and Tibet have born the brunt of the Han heavy-handedness. China has ruled these two restive regions through an excessively oppressive colonization that includes cultural genocide. China has purposefully flooded the two regions with Han migrants, thus, completely reshaping the local demographics. And it has put draconian restrictions on the freedom and religions of the local natives, restrictions such as not being allowed to pray, not being allowed to build places of worship, not being allowed to grow facial hair, not being allowed to wear certain clothing, not being allowed to congregate, being forced to show loyalty to the CPC, and being forced to hand in their passports.

China always tries to keep the outside world from knowing of its transgressions in Xinjiang and Tibet by barring foreign media access and by placing restrictions on foreign tourists; however, China's harsh treatment of the locals is well documented. In one example of egregious oppression, an Uighur professor of economics at one of Beijing's best universities was jailed for life, even though he was a moderate, because he advocated some very basic rights for the Uighurs.

The fact is that in Xinjiang, Uighur areas have been placed under martial law with heavy armed police presence

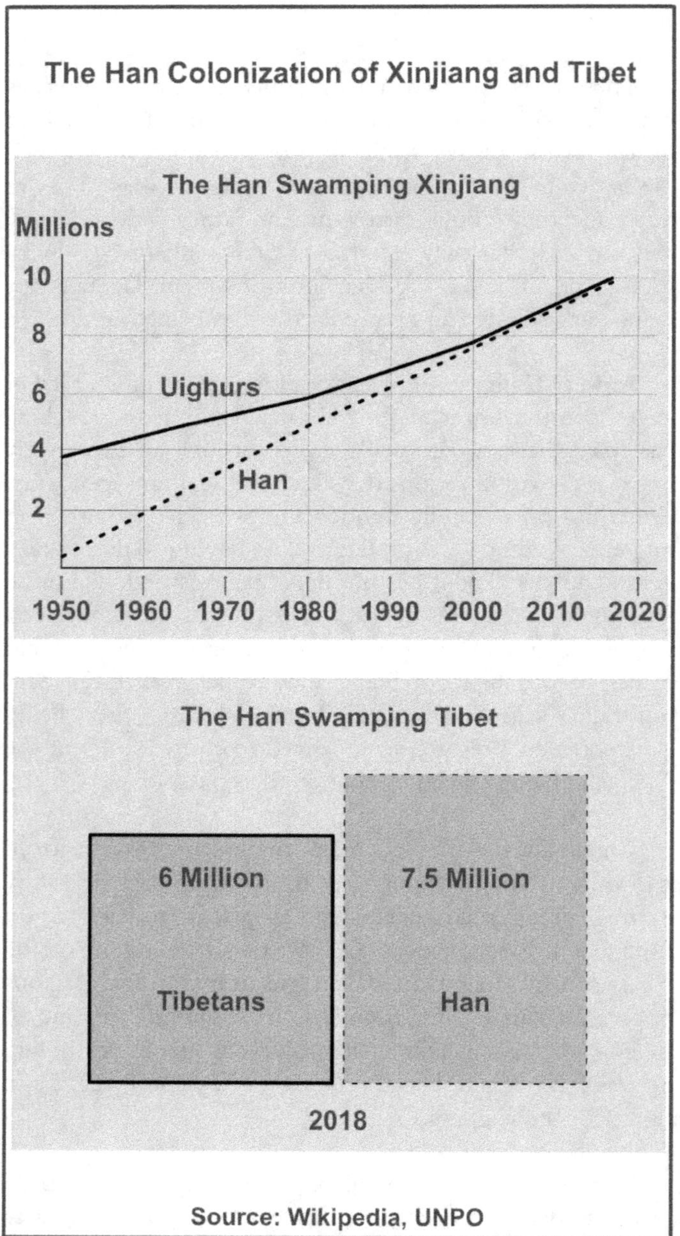
The Han Colonization of Xinjiang and Tibet
The Han Swamping Xinjiang
Millions
10
8
6
4
2
Uighurs
Han
1950 1960 1970 1980 1990 2000 2010 2020
The Han Swamping Tibet
6 Million
Tibetans
7.5 Million
Han
2018
Source: Wikipedia, UNPO

everywhere, mass surveillance, restrictions on religious practice, restrictions on movement, restrictions on gatherings, mass DNA collection, and political reeducation camps. In August 2018, a United Nations human rights panel said it had received credible evidence that China had turned the Uighur autonomous region into a massive internment camp, and almost a million Uighurs were being held indefinitely without charge, poorly fed, and tortured. In 2019, US Assistant Secretary of Defense Randall Schriver told a Pentagon briefing that "The Communist Party (of China) is using the security forces for mass imprisonment of Chinese Muslims in concentration camps," estimating that the number of detained Muslims could be "closer to 3 million citizens." These prisoners are being forcefully reeducated to give up their religion and language. They are forced to shout CPC slogans, and swear loyalty to the CPC and Xi Jinping. In July 2019, US Secretary of State Mike Pompeo called China's treatment of its Uighur Muslim minority the "stain of the century."

China, true to its lying antics, has denied the whole matter. However, satellite imagery and testimonies of escapees from the camps have clearly shown that there were political reeducation camps that China had built to imprison millions of Uighurs. Despite the overwhelming and clear evidence, China has kept lying as it always does, and said that these were vocational schools! Vocational schools for whole families? Vocational schools for a whole ethnic group? The Chinese lying and deception know no limit.

China is oppressing its Muslim minority not only in Xinjiang but also in other parts of China. In the northwestern autonomous province of Ningxia, the home of millions of Hui Muslims, the Chinese government crackdown on Muslims has continued, with the latest incident being the forcible demolition of a major mosque in 2018. According to the government, the mosque didn't have the proper building permits but that's nonsense because the mosque took two years to build, time during which the government could've stopped construction but didn't. The real reason is that China under Xi has declared Muslims as enemies of the state. China has even declared war on Arabic-sounding names of places in the Muslim areas of Ningxia and Xinjiang.

As for Tibet, China has radically altered this roof-of-the-world territory. China carved out one area of that territory and called it the Tibet "Autonomous" Region (TAR), and parceled out the rest of the territory into pieces that it incorporated into the provinces of Qinghai, Gansu, Sichuan and Yunnan. The Tibet shown on modern China's maps is just the TAR.

China has committed cultural genocide against the Tibetan people with heavy police and military oppression, destruction of monasteries, restrictions on religion, forced education in the Chinese language, forced resettlements, land expropriation, and by flooding the territory with Han immigrants. China's oppressive occupation has led many Tibetans to utter despair, to the point of self-immolation.

China's ruthless occupation of Tibet is implacably intransigent. Indeed, China even considers the Dalai Lama, a holy and peaceful monk, to be the devil himself. The CPC is so hell-bent on controlling Tibet that it decided that only it could vet and anoint the next Dalai Lama. This is beyond belief. How can atheists decide the succession process of a religion?

The extent of China's ironhanded rule can be seen in the fact that China even threatens other countries that dare to welcome the Dalai Lama in any kind of capacity. In some ways, one could argue that what China is doing to the Tibetans and Uighurs is a prelude to what it will do to the rest of the world.

China's jingoism and belligerence

China has in recent years shown its true colors, that of being a rising nationalist and belligerent power. For a long time, while it was economically and militarily weak, it hid its agenda and played the role of a pacifist country. It didn't even acknowledge its rise as a power. It wanted the world's attention to be focused elsewhere while it built up its economy and military. It followed the directive of the late paramount leader Deng Xiaoping to "Hide our strength, and bide our time." Unfortunately for the rest of the world, China's strategy has succeeded, and now China is no longer shy about talking about its rise and pushing its agenda of ultimate world dominance.

In today's China, jingoism is the order of the day. Fanned by unrelenting communist propaganda, China's jingoism has reached alarming levels. It's gotten to the point where the Chinese, who used to be meek and deferential to Westerners, are now openly hostile and antagonistic toward foreigners, especially Westerners. They seem to have a chip on their shoulder, and are eager to flaunt their newfound confidence and power.

One example of China's alarming jingoism came after an international tribunal, the Permanent Court of Arbitration in the Hague, ruled in 2016 that China's claims to the South China Sea were bogus, that China's famous nine-dash line had no historical or legal validity, and that China had grossly violated the territorial sovereignty of the Philippines. China became incensed, declared that it wouldn't abide by the ruling even though it was legally bound by it, and let loose its hordes of fanatic jingoists who went even further and vented their anger not only on the Philippines by demanding among other things a boycott of that Southeast Asian country's products such as mangoes and bananas, but also on the US, which they accused of being the fomenter of the whole affair. These Chinese jingoists boisterously demonstrated against the US and held demonstrations near KFC and McDonald's outlets, which they saw as symbols of the US government. The demonstrators held signs that called for these food franchises to get out of China.

Many Chinese were seen in online video forums smashing their iPhones because in their senseless minds Apple was a representative of US imperialism. Some Chinese companies urged their employees to get rid of their iPhones and offered to compensate them. Some companies threatened to fire any employee who bought a new iPhone, while others declared that anyone caught with a new iPhone would never be promoted. And in one example that bordered on the ridiculous, a Chinese guy wearing Nike shoes was attacked by other Chinese in a subway because Nike's an American company!

China's jingoism has also manifested itself in many other forms and on many other occasions. Thus, when tensions flared up with Japan after the latter bought the Senkaku Islands from a private Japanese owner, not only did diplomatic relations between the two countries deteriorate, but there were also many street demonstrations against the Japanese, calls for boycotts of Japanese goods, and public displays of Japan hatred, such as the smashing of Japanese cars. And when South Korea deployed an American missile defense system to defend itself against the rogue regime of North Korea, the same jingoistic manifestations happened again and included among other things the cancellation of Chinese tour groups to Korea, the cancellation of cultural exchanges, and the public smashing of Samsung electrical appliances.

Sometimes China's jingoism borders on the absurd. Indeed, the Chinese government is so sensitive about maps of China that it doesn't tolerate any map of China that doesn't include Taiwan, Hong Kong, Tibet and the South China Sea as parts of it. Recently, book publishers selling in China had to stop including maps of China for fear of running afoul of the Chinese authorities. Even the US clothing retailer Gap was denounced by the Chinese for making a T-shirt showing only mainland China. Gap had to issue an official apology to China for not including Taiwan and the South China Sea as being part of China. The crazy thing was that the shirt was for sale in North America and not in China.

Chinese jingoism manifests itself even far from the mainland. Thus, some Chinese organize trips to Japan's Senkaku Islands, and manage to land on them and plant the Chinese flag before being forcibly removed by the Japanese coast guard. Some Chinese fishing boats caught illegally fishing in the territorial waters of neighboring countries, such as Japan and South Korea, are so aggressive as to ram the coast guard ships of those countries.

Nowadays, the Chinese overseas have become more and more truculent. In one incident that happened in Thailand, after their plane was delayed for hours, a horde of Chinese tourists became very defiant, started singing the Chinese national anthem and refused to board the plane. Another example was that some Chinese workers in the Gambia in Africa planted the Chinese flag as a form of defiance and superiority to the locals. And another example is seeing the Chinese congregate on Cambodia's beaches and play loud Chinese patriotic songs proclaiming their pride, their rise, and seemingly their newfound status

Everybody Must Apologize to China

The following companies had to apologize to China
for what were really frivolous reasons, such as
quoting the Dalai Lama,
showing a China map without the South China Sea,
using chopsticks in ads,
talking about Chinese pigs,
and so on:

Mercedes-Benz   Zara   Apple   Versace   Fresh

UBS   Calvin Klein   Quantas   Gap

Coach   Swarovski   Marriott   Valentino

Delta   Medtronic   McDonald's   MAC

Pocari Sweat   Asics   Givenchy

Dolce & Gabbana   ...

as colonizers.

In their gung-ho jingoism, the Chinese have become so brainwashed and arrogant as to reject historical facts. Once, while discussing a topic with his students, an American English professor in Beijing mentioned a relevant example of how Japan used to occupy parts of China. One of the Chinese students immediately became all riled up because he didn't accept that Japan ever occupied China. When the professor tried to explain that Japan did occupy parts of China and even settled some parts of Manchuria in the northeast of China, the Chinese student became even more incensed, and threatened to contact the school administration about the incident! The professor tried to patiently and reasonably explain himself, but the student was utterly unmoved and very antagonistic.

China's rise is manifested not only in its virulent jingoism but also in the dramatic change of its foreign policy. China's oft-repeated lies about its peaceful rise have finally been laid to rest as the world has plainly witnessed the emergence of an unequivocally belligerent China, a power that's an existential threat to many countries, even to the US in the not-so-distant future.

China's belligerence can be seen in the words of its top diplomat, State Councilor and ex foreign minister Yang Jiechi, who when asked about China's claim to almost all of the South China Sea to the detriment of Southeast Asian countries said, "China is a big country and other countries are small countries, and that is just a fact." Such Chinese thinking has precedents in Mao Zedong's saying that "Political power grows out of the barrel of a gun," and Deng Xiaoping's directive to "Hide our strength, and bide our time."

China is no longer afraid to show its true self, that of a

ruthless, power-hungry, and belligerent power whose ultimate goal is to recreate the world order of centuries past when the Middle Kingdom was the center of global power and other countries were its tributaries.

One undeniable fact is that the Chinese, politicians and others, have proven time and again to be far from sincere in any dealings or pronouncements about their intentions, whether political, economic, or military. Even US president Trump knew full well of the Chinese propensity for lying through their teeth when he said, "No surprise that China was caught cheating in the Olympics. That's the Chinese MO: Lie, Cheat and Steal in all international dealings."

The list of Chinese flagrant lies and deceptions is very long. One prominent example is that during his 2015 trip to Washington, Chinese supreme leader Xi Jinping publicly stated that China wouldn't militarize the artificial islands that it was building in the South China Sea. However, soon thereafter satellite imagery showed that China had installed comprehensive weapons systems on those islands, systems that included radar stations and anti-aircraft guns. These fortifications were in addition to the building of military-length airstrips and ports to harbor warships. China has converted those artificial islands into what are been called "unsinkable aircraft carriers."

The evidence of China's belligerent rise has been there for the whole world to see, but somehow the world has been either blind or too afraid to do much about it. Perhaps one of the best telling examples of China's bellicose rise happened during the run-up to the Beijing Olympics of 2008 when the Olympic torch was carried all over the world, and China used some of its security goons to escort it with force through demonstrating crowds. Those goons pushed and punched their way through

Lying Chinese

It seems that just as most Chinese can't drive well,
they also have a problem being honest.
Here are three of their thousands of lies:

Xi says	Xi does
China will not militarize the South China Sea islands	China has militarized them with surface-to-air missiles, anti-ship cruise missiles, radar stations, hangars for fighter jets, and shelters for mobile missile launchers
China will stop economic cyber espionage	China not only didn't stop its espionage, but it also expanded it
China will not dominate any country	China has used predatory economics to subjugate countries all over the world

peaceful demonstrators in many countries. This thuggery that marred the peaceful spirit of the Olympics was vividly captured in imagery that shocked the world. The thugs' behavior was a clear demonstration of the Chinese character, of things to come, and of how China would bully its way around the world.

China has lied. China has deceived. And China has risen. China played the West and other countries beautifully with its lies about a peaceful rise. China conned the rest of the world into going along with its lies while feverishly building up its economic and military might. And China has succeeded. China now acts as a self-assured economic superpower and a rising military superpower whose motto is "Might is right."

The belligerent China has in the last few years been stamping its hegemony over many parts of the world. In the Yellow Sea, China pushed South Korea to yield more of the sea to it because it argued that it's the bigger country in both area and population. China used its economic leverage and military might to bully South Korea.

In the East China Sea, China is pushing Japan to the limit. China claims sovereignty over Japan's Senkaku Islands and is constantly and aggressively patrolling near or intruding in the waters and airspace of those islands, thus, forcing Japan to be on constant alert and to regularly scramble coast guard ships and fighter jets. China's military aircraft, warships and submarines have also engaged in provocative maneuvers and intrusions near Japan's main islands. China is unilaterally drilling for and pumping out natural gas from gas fields that belong to both countries. And China has even challenged Japan's sovereignty over Okinawa! China's transgressions have been so egregious that Japan, a peace-loving country since the end of World War II, had to start amending its pacifist constitution to deal with the Chinese military threat.

In the South China Sea, China has brazenly claimed sovereignty over most of that sea and has been actively enforcing its claim. China's dubious claim, known as the nine-dash line, is so outrageous as to be laughable, for it even includes the territorial waters of Malaysia, which are a thousand miles away from China. And even though the Permanent Court of Arbitration ruled in 2016 that China's nine-dash-line claim had no legal basis, China continues its militarization of that sea.

According to the US Department of Defense, China has reclaimed more than 3,000 acres through the massive dredging of Fiery Cross, Subi, Mischief, Cuarteron, Gaven, and Hughes reefs in the Spratly Islands. China has built up these artificial islands into military bases with runways and hangars for military aircraft, ports for warships, shelters for missiles, radar stations, and anti-aircraft guns.

China's belligerence in the South China Sea has reached alarming levels, for even US warships and planes peacefully and legally patrolling in that area have been confronted. Indeed, China's navy has harassed US Navy ships in the South China Sea by shadowing them, blocking their path, warning them to leave, destroying their towed sonar arrays, and even stealing one of their underwater drones in plain sight. US Navy reconnaissance planes that fly in international airspace over the South China Sea, and the East China Sea also, are routinely intercepted and harassed by Chinese fighter jets that make dangerously close passes and perform stunts like barrel rolls over them.

With regards to Taiwan, China has used a three-pronged strategy to eventually subjugate that island. On the economic front, China has increased its economic leverage and put an economic noose around that island

China The Bully
China
8
9
7
6
5
1
2
3
4
1 Bullying South Korea
2 Bullying Japan
3 Bullying Taiwan
4 Bullying Southeast Asia
5 Bullying Bhutan
6 Bullying India
7 Oppressing Tibetans
8 Oppressing Uighurs
9 Bullying Mongolia

through trade and huge investments. On the political front, China has effectively isolated Taiwan by whittling down the number of countries that still recognized Taiwan, and by excluding Taiwan from international conferences and institutions like the World Health Organization. On the military front, China not only keeps hundreds of missiles pointed at Taiwan and keeps training for amphibious landings on that island, but it also has developed enough of an interdiction capability to keep the US from militarily intervening during a conflict. And as a constant reminder to Taiwan, China regularly conducts war maneuvers by its navy and air force in Taiwan's vicinity and around it.

And around the world, China is propping up economically and militarily Third World dictatorships and pariah states like North Korea. Tens of dictatorships in Africa, Asia and Latin America would be swept off power if it weren't for such Chinese support.

China is undermining the UN and NGOs' human-rights efforts around the world, such as when it bullied the Thai government into forcibly repatriating tens of Uighur refugees back to China even though the UN explicitly said those people were genuine refugees. China ignores international institutions, such as the Permanent Court of Arbitration, when they don't suit it. China wants to be the only emerging power on the UN Security Council, and doesn't want to expand this international body and make it more representative of the world by including worthy candidates like India. China uses the UN Security Council to protect and further its interests, and to punish unfriendly countries. For example, in the case of Macedonia, China vetoed a UN Security Council resolution to keep badly needed UN peacekeepers in Macedonia because that country established diplomatic relations with Taiwan. China threatens and punishes countries that call for the respect of human rights in China, such as when it banned salmon imports from Norway and refused a visa for a former Norwegian prime minister, all because the Nobel Peace Prize committee based in Norway awarded the Nobel Peace Prize to a Chinese dissident. China threatens and punishes countries that host visits by the Dalai Lama. China even bullies the tiniest of countries in the world, such as Bhutan, which China has been pushing to make territorial concessions.

And the list of China's belligerent activities keeps growing with its rise, regardless of the target. Thus, China is no longer afraid of taking on the US directly, whether in its near seas or faraway. Indeed, according to Pentagon sources, Chinese fishermen, who actually double up as China's maritime militia and are called its Little Blue Men, have been flashing lasers at American military planes flying not only near China in the East China Sea and South China Sea, but also as far away as Africa, in Djibouti. These laserings use commercial and military-grade lasers, and are aimed to injure aircraft pilots. And what was the US response to these blatant acts of war? Well, even the hawkish Trump administration cowed under and only responded by delivering a formal diplomatic protest requesting China to investigate. China, as could be expected, denied responsibility for these attacks.

Pax Sinica

The center of global economic, political and military power is gradually but surely moving away from the West and toward China. Pax Americana is waning and China's influence is rising. While US and Western leaders keep naively and moronically talking of engagement and win-win strategies with China, Chinese leaders have all along engaged in a global zero-sum game that they expect to win at the expense of the West.

On every continent China is winning. In America, political squabbling, stalemate, venality, levity, and even stupidity have irrevocably wrecked the country and set it on a course to decline and irrelevance. US leaders are either afraid of antagonizing China, naïve about China's intentions, or simply incompetent. One example of the US utter stupidity in dealing with China is that the US has for years and years enlisted China's help to rein in North Korea. This US policy is beyond insane. China is the one that helped North Korea in the Korean War. China is the one that helped North Korea with its nuclear program. China is the one that is solely propping up the North Korean economy. China doesn't want a unified Korea with US soldiers on its doorstep. China needs North Korea as a buffer against US troops. China wants the US out of the Korean peninsula and out of the whole of East Asia. And yet, US leaders think that China will take their side against North Korea. How stupid are they?

In any case, the state of affairs in America has become so rotten that many prominent Americans in many fields have sold out to China. These shamelessly dishonorable scabs support China and lobby for it at the expense of their own country. They include senators, congressmen, Speakers of the House, Secretaries of State, Secretaries of the Treasury, from left and right, even paragons of American conservatism and "patriotism." In their blind quest to earn small fortunes, which China happily pays, these Americans have whored themselves to the China money machine and sold out their country.

Before Trump came to power, China had effectively neutered the US. Trump has shown signs of being a true patriot by defending America's interests and standing up to China. Any hope of America stopping the Chinese menace rests with whether Trump maintains his hawkish stance toward China.

Just like America, Europe has lacked any resolve to stand up to China. China knows how to neutralize and manipulate the weak, divided, and rudderless continent of Europe by investing billions of dollars in its various countries, which then become beholden to China and defend it in European and international forums. European leaders are so afraid of losing Chinese money that they have abandoned their principles and willingly kowtow to Beijing. They accommodate China such as by not bringing up the issue of human rights, not dealing with the Dalai Lama, and engaging in a myriad of other obsequious acts.

The perfect example is that of Greece, the spineless country that has whored itself to China in exchange for Chinese investments such as the hundreds of millions of dollars in the Greek port of Piraeus in which China's Cosco now controls a 2/3 stake. In 2016, Greece opposed an EU statement critical of China's regional expansionism in the South China Sea. And in 2017, Greece blocked a European Union statement at the United Nations that was critical of China's human rights record.

China's designs on Europe have reached alarmingly audacious levels. Indeed, China has in recent years targeted the big island of Greenland for its conquest by investing in its mines and offering to build huge airports for that island, whose total population of about 56,000 people isn't even as big as a small US town. China is pushing these economic projects, and is stealthily and gradually pushing for Greenland's independence from Denmark, knowing full well that such a huge and poor country with a tiny population would be a perfect target for its predatory economics. China's nefarious intentions on Greenland became apparent in 2016 when a Chinese company registered in Hong Kong tried to buy an old naval base in Greenland, but was fortunately turned down by Denmark. This Chinese attempt reminds one of China's other major deceptive coup when it acquired its first-aircraft-carrier hull from the Ukraine by categorizing that acquisition as purely economic when in truth the Chinese military was behind it.

Even the Vatican caved in to China. In 2018, the Vatican signed an agreement with China on the appointment of bishops. The bishops in China will have to be vetted and proposed by the CPC, an atheist body, before being approved by the Pope!

Africa is already in China's pocket. Since virtually all African countries are dictatorships, they fall in line nicely with China, which under the guise of not interfering into other countries' internal affairs props them up and grooms them into satellites. China already has a naval base in Djibouti, and it can easily open more bases on that continent whenever it pleases. One example of China's influence is that when Zimbabwe's army decided to force the long-serving president Mugabe out of power, the head of the military flew to Beijing, not Washington or some European capital, to get the OK for the move.

In Latin America, China has cultivated close ties with Cuba, Nicaragua, Venezuela, Brazil and others. Using its economic clout and huge investments, China will keep on building up its influence in Latin America at the expense of the US.

In Oceania, China's huge investments and big trade with Australia, New Zealand and others have already yielded great political benefits to China. These countries now see their future as more tied to Asia in general and China in particular than to the West. Whereas in the past, these countries used to toe the US line, now they have to carefully balance their policies whenever China is involved.

One example that illustrates China's newfound nefarious influence in Australia happened in 2017 when a major Australian publisher, Allen & Unwin, was accused by an Australian professor of reneging on an agreement to publish his book because apparently the book was critical of China. The professor said that the publisher was concerned that his book, titled *Silent Invasion: How China is Turning Australia into a Puppet State*, may cause some defamation actions. The professor noted that "This really is a watershed in the debate over China's suppression of free speech." He continued that "It is the first instance where a major Western publisher has decided to censor material of the Chinese Communist Party in its home country."

Australia has been swamped by hordes of Chinese immigrants. Australia's 2017 census results show that it is increasingly an Asian nation, with Asian migration outstripping that of Europeans for the first time and Mandarin now the second-most spoken language after English.

And the Chinese nefarious presence has already shaken Australia. Thus, most Sydney residents believe that the Chinese should not be allowed to buy property in the city because the Chinese are making life miserable for Australians when it comes to housing. According to CNBC, in the Australian state of New South Wales where Sydney is located, foreign buyers, 87% of whom were Chinese, bought a quarter of new property supply and raised the market to levels that priced out local buyers. The Chinese have also bought up many of Australia's businesses and farmland, and China is now racing past all other countries to become the biggest owner of Australia's farmland. The Chinese even control the harbor of Darwin.

Australia is slowly sliding in China's orbit, and the Australians have seen first hand that the Chinese will always be Chinese. Thus, Chinese Australians and their media always side with China, such as on the South China Sea issue, to the detriment of Australia, and work hard to change Australia's foreign policy to be in line with that of China.

The Chinese have so much infiltrated and influenced Australia that this country had to pass in 2018 a national security legislation that was squarely aimed at the Chinese threat. The Chinese immigrants and investors that have been invading Australia in huge numbers in recent years owe allegiance to China before Australia. For example, a Chinese billionaire and Australia resident by the name of Huang Xiangmo, who applied for Australian citizenship, rescinded a pledge of a large donation to Australia's Labor Party because he was upset that a Labor official said that Australia should help the US and send naval patrols to the South China Sea.

China's nefarious activities in Oceania reach even the tiniest of countries. Thus, in the case of the Pacific island of Palau, which continues to maintain ties with Taiwan, China barred its tourists from visiting that island. Since the hordes of Chinese tourists accounted for half of the tourists to Palau, the effect has been devastating to that island's economy, which relies heavily on tourism. China's ban has resulted in shuttered travel agencies, idle tour boats, empty hotel rooms, empty restaurants, and idle construction sites that the Chinese had bought. And the egregious fact is that China engineered this wicked scenario. Indeed, China first allowed this tourist boom in Palau with the backhanded goal of making Palau dependent on it and forcing it to sever ties with Taiwan.

When Palau didn't give in, China pulled the plug on the tourist dollars to Palau.

And in Asia, China is winning big, not only to the detriment of the West, but also to that of Japan and India. China has been able to dominate Asia through economic initiatives like the One Belt One Road initiative, and political treaties like the Shanghai Security Alliance.

Central Asian countries, which are majority Muslim, are now so heavily dependent on Chinese trade and investments that they collude with China in its oppression of fellow Muslims in Xinjiang. South Asian countries, except for India, have developed very close political, economic, and military ties with China. West Asian countries are big suppliers of oil and gas to China, and China's influence in those countries is growing with its huge investments. And Southeast Asian countries have been one by one gradually but surely succumbing to Chinese influence, even though the South China Sea dispute remains a very thorny issue. Thus, in Thailand, the military junta has stayed in power for years and instituted new constitutional changes that make the concept of democracy in Thailand a joke. The junta doesn't heed any Western complaints because China provides the necessary financial and political support. And in Myanmar, the leader, a political whore of China, has shown her true face and condoned the ethnic cleansing committed against the Rohingya. This woman disputed the clear and overwhelming evidence provided by the UN and NGOs that clearly indicated the atrocities committed by the Burmese military and the Buddhist militias, and turned a deaf ear to Western calls for justice because China provided her with the political and financial backing she needed. Thus, in 2018, when the UN Human Rights Council voted to investigate Myanmar for human rights abuses against 700,000 Rohingya, abuses including ethnic cleansing and genocide, China voted against the move.

The dawn of Pax Sinica is upon the world, and a perfect example of how the world will be reshaped under China can be seen in today's Cambodia, a country that welcomed China with open arms and paid the ultimate price of being basically bought up and turned into a quasi-colony. This is not a misstatement, and here are the facts. Cambodia has become China's third colony after Xinjiang and Tibet because the answers to the following questions are all in the affirmative:

1. Have huge numbers of Chinese recently settled in Cambodia?
2. Have the Chinese taken over the best places in Cambodia?
3. Are the Chinese treated better than the locals by the Cambodian government?
4. Is Cambodia mainly dependent on China economically and militarily?
5. Is the Cambodian government a puppet regime of China?

The answers to these questions are now detailed.

First, yes, many Chinese have recently settled in Cambodia. In 2018, according to Cambodia's Ministry of Tourism there were over 2 million Chinese visitors in Cambodia, a small country with a population of only 16 million people, and about half a million Chinese have recently settled permanently in Cambodia. These numbers are expected to swell even more dramatically to 5 million by 2025 and 8 million by 2030. They have bought and rented for decades all kinds of properties, and intend on staying forever. The number of these settlers is increasing daily and rapidly as the Chinese, in their usual way, bring in more Chinese: family members, relatives, friends,

China's Third Colony

Cambodia has become China's third colony, after Xinjiang and Tibet.

Source: Phnom Penh Post, Khmer Times, The Guardian

acquaintances, workers and clans. All kinds of Chinese are rushing in, not just the investors, but also laborers, farmers, all kinds of workers, and whole families.

These Chinese have settled everywhere in Cambodia, even in the remotest of places. Walking in the capital Phnom Penh and the main coastal city of Sihanoukville, one cannot but be amazed by the scale of the Chinese takeover. These two cities, and countless other places in the country, are awash with Chinese-language posters, and peppered with Chinese-owned establishments and projects.

No other place has been invaded like Sihanoukville, the main port of Cambodia. Sihanoukville, once a sleepy seedy port popular with Western backpackers and tourists, has been transformed into a bustling Chinese casino city. Every street, alley, road, and corner has been taken over by the Chinese, and casinos are everywhere, some 80 according to some estimates. Such complete is the Chinese takeover that Sihanoukville has been nicknamed *Macau II*, *New Macau*, and *Chinatown*. The word *Chinatown* isn't really appropriate here because usually *Chinatown* refers to a part of a city outside of China that has been settled by the Chinese; however, in this case the whole city is *Chinatown*. The long-serving Cambodian strongman called Sihanoukville the *Dragon head* of Cambodia.

The number of Chinese in Sihanoukville increased sharply. Indeed, back in 2014, Sihanoukville was popular with Western tourists, and the Chinese were nowhere to be seen except outside the city in a Special Economic Zone. And then came the deluge as the Chinese hordes rushed in. In 2018, after just four years, the Chinese made up more than half of the city's population and Westerners became a rarity. In Sihanoukville's Special Economic Zone, 150 out of 160 companies are Chinese.

Sihanoukville is now truly a Chinese city. Such is their overwhelming presence that during the Chinese New Year when many Chinese return to China to visit relatives, Sihanoukville becomes eerily quiet.

Second, yes, the Chinese have taken over the best places in Cambodia. The Chinese now have control of Cambodia's beaches and most of the coast, and in other places of the country the cash-flush Chinese get anything they want because money talks and the corrupt local government is only too willing to take bribes.

Cambodia's best places are arguably its coastal areas and nice beaches, and the Chinese have acquired them. The Chinese firm Union Development Group (UDG) has a 99-year lease on a huge concession of 45,000 hectares that encompasses almost 20% of Cambodia's entire coastline on the Gulf of Thailand. This concession, when granted a few years back, had corruption written all over it as not only did it break Cambodian law, which limited concessions to 10,000 hectares, but it also included parceling off a large part of the protected Botum Sakor National Park, a fact which required a royal decree. This almost $4 billion concession, called Dara Sakor Beachside Resort, is being developed as a new Chinese city in Cambodia. The Chinese plan to build condominiums, hotels, hospitals, casinos, golf courses, an airport, and very importantly a deep-sea port that will eventually serve as a Chinese naval base.

This concession in the province of Koh Kong near the Thai border involved the land confiscation and the eviction of poor indigenous people. The Chinese company used the Cambodian government security forces and military to forcibly remove the local people. These locals, mainly poor fishing families, resisted and their homes were bulldozed and burned down. After being evicted, these fishermen who had lived in the area for generations were taken inland far away from the coast and told that they were now farmers. They were given new plots of land, but those plots were so infertile that they couldn't grow anything.

With their possessions in the provinces of Koh Kong and Sihanouk, the Chinese control more than half of the Cambodian coast. Now they have set their sights on Kampot to complete their takeover of Cambodia's whole coast.

It's truly a shame that the Chinese control the beaches of Cambodia because they don't like suntanning. They're always trying to avoid the sun and to have as fair a complexion as possible! These days when walking the beautiful beaches of Sihanoukville on beautiful sunny days, one is eerily struck by how they are almost totally deserted compared to years before when Westerners thronged there for sun and fun.

Third, yes, the Chinese are treated better than the locals by the Cambodian government. The locals have become second-class citizens to the Chinese as far as the government is concerned. Indeed, whatever the Chinese want, they get.

When the Chinese break the law, the national government has instructed the police and courts to treat them with kid gloves. In disputes between the Chinese and the Khmers, the Cambodian government has also instructed the police and courts to favor the Chinese. Thus, when the Chinese beat the Khmers or torch their businesses or cheat them in business transactions, the police and courts don't do much.

The mistreatment of the local population for the

benefit of the Chinese has affected many locals. Thus, in order to accommodate Chinese demand for land to develop or farm or log, tens of thousands of poor Cambodians have been forcibly removed from their lands by corrupt officials for paltry compensation or none at all. And the Chinese, as is their usual habit with regards to the environment, do not particularly care about Cambodia's farmland and forests. Huge tracts of farmland that was acquired through corrupt officials has been turned into real estate development areas, or changed from rice fields to sugar cane plantations. And forests are being illegally logged and their timber, especially the expensive rosewood, is being shipped to China.

One example of the clear favoritism of the Chinese is in Sihanouk province where power and water cuts have become very frequent as the Chinese have swamped the area, and during such times the electricity and water are prioritized toward the Chinese areas to the detriment of the fewer and fewer locals.

One sickening example of how many Cambodians have become second-class citizens in their own country is seeing them holding umbrellas for the Chinese as the latter come out of establishments, such as casinos, for a walk. As these Chinese walk leisurely down the street, the Khmer helpers, or rather servants, follow along holding the umbrellas to shield them from the sun. This sickening sight happens with both male and female, young and old Chinese.

And the Cambodian government favors the Chinese over the locals even though the Chinese have brought many problems to Cambodia. Indeed, letting loose hundreds of thousands of Chinese in a country like Cambodia where laws are lax and corruption is rampant has created a Wild West that the Chinese have turned into a playground for their uncivilized behavior and criminal acts. In their home country the Chinese are tamed by the iron-handed control of their government, but in Cambodia the Chinese are running wild and wreaking havoc on the local population, culture, economy, and environment.

The list of Chinese problems is long and includes money laundering in the billions of dollars, large-scale prostitution, illegal gambling, drugs, fighting, rudeness, noise, pollution, garbage, hawking, spitting, bad driving, drunk driving, driving without a license, Internet scams, phone scams, human trafficking, ethnic tension, kidnappings of both Chinese and Khmer nationals, gang rapes of Khmer girls, huge forced displacement and takeover of both Khmer and Western businesses, loansharking, fake goods, illegal logging, smuggling, widespread corruption of the civilian and military institutions, bribing of officials, absconding without paying employee wages, illegally working, not declaring income, evading taxes, and the list goes on.

In the case of prostitution, thousands of Chinese prostitutes have flooded Cambodia, especially the big cities. They can be found in hotels, spas, massage parlors, KTVs and other places. They and their Chinese pimps advertise their services with sex leaflets on beaches, building entrances, trees, electric poles, and many other places. They also offer their services online, such as on the popular social media WeChat.

In the case of drugs, the Chinese smuggle in huge amounts from China and other places. One Chinese was nabbed for importing 100kg of ecstasy pills from Germany.

In the case of pollution, wherever the Chinese settle, pollution follows. Thus, in Sihanoukville there's so much construction that air pollution has become a major health

The Chinese Exporting their Corrupt Ways

IP Theft

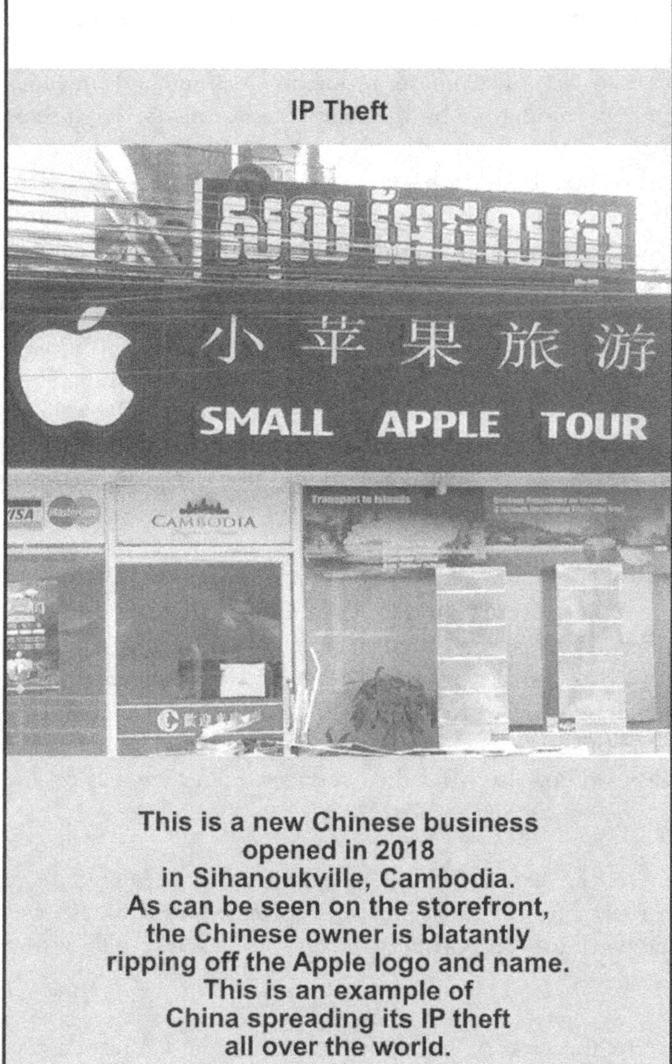

This is a new Chinese business
opened in 2018
in Sihanoukville, Cambodia.
As can be seen on the storefront,
the Chinese owner is blatantly
ripping off the Apple logo and name.
This is an example of
China spreading its IP theft
all over the world.

problem. Gone are the days of blue skies and fresh air.

In the case of the displacement of Khmers and Westerners, the Chinese use their huge amounts of illicit money and people to their advantage. For example, the Chinese offer more money to Khmer landlords to kick out Western and Khmer tenants from their establishments and then the Chinese cram these establishments with their hordes, living like animals, often with six or more Chinese in an apartment that previously housed one Westerner.

And in the case of Internet scams, one such scam uses Chinese females to befriend girls online and get their naked pictures, and then use those naked pictures to extort money from them. Cambodian police have arrested and deported thousands of Chinese nationals over Internet scams, such as VoIP ones.

The Chinese have created so many problems and crime that even the governor of Sihanouk province, a Chinese Khmer who's really more Chinese than Khmer and who greatly facilitated the Chinese invasion of his province, complained publicly. Still, even though the Chinese commit more crime in Cambodia than any other foreigners, the country's strongman, himself of Chinese heritage, asked the local authorities not to talk about it publicly!

Even though Chinese investment has brought wealth to Cambodia, this wealth is mainly kept within Cambodia's Chinese community. Chinese residents and visitors in Cambodia buy from Chinese businesses, eat in Chinese restaurants, stay in Chinese hotels, and of course gamble in Chinese casinos. The trickle-down effect to Khmer businesses is minimal, and the only beneficiaries are the landowners, many of whom are of Chinese ancestry anyway, and who rented or sold their land to new Chinese arrivals.

Perhaps an early harbinger of bad things to come from the Chinese was the Kamchay dam, the first large-scale Chinese investment project in Cambodia. The dam's construction destroyed thousands of hectares of forest, threatened wildlife, and lowered water quality, consequences that adversely affected the livelihoods of local communities.

Fourth, yes, Cambodia is mainly dependent on China economically and militarily. China has become Cambodia's largest trading partner, largest provider of foreign aid, and largest source of foreign direct investment. Chinese companies, state-owned and private, big and small, have invested billions of dollars in the country setting up all kinds of businesses, such as textile factories and sugar mills, and building up all types of infrastructure, including highways, railway, bridges, dams, and power plants, all for the greater benefit of the Chinese.

And the Chinese investments have gone even deeper in penetrating the fabric of the local economy and having a major impact on the Cambodian society. Thus, the Chinese have bought and taken over local guesthouses, hotels, and residential buildings. The Chinese have also built their own real estate properties, including entire apartment complexes and resorts for themselves, usually using Chinese workers. The Chinese have also bought and built shops, supermarkets, restaurants, KTVs, spas, and massage parlors that cater mainly to Chinese customers. They have set up investment offices to help their fellow countrymen, and travel agencies with their own Chinese tour guides. They have built many new casinos for visiting Chinese gamblers, and also rented guesthouses that they illegally use to operate online live dealer casinos for customers back in China. They even brought their own goons to enforce their presence and guard their establishments, such as hotels, casinos, KTVs, and massage parlors. Not only are the Chinese present everywhere in Cambodia, but together with the Chinese Khmers they also overwhelmingly control the economy.

The Chinese takeover of Cambodia has had a big negative impact on Western expatriates and tourists in Cambodia whose way of life has been severely disrupted. Westerners, who used to live in or go to places like Sihanoukville to enjoy the beaches or Siem Reap to visit Angkor Wat, are now fewer and fewer because the Chinese have totally changed the character of those places with their hordes, noise, rude manners, and the jacking up of the prices of everything from food to accommodations.

China now also completely controls the Cambodian military. The Chinese have built complete bases and barracks for the Cambodian armed forces, and trained their officers both locally and in China. China has also supplied the Cambodian army with jeeps, trucks, helicopters, rocket launchers, and uniforms. The Chinese and Cambodian armed forces now hold regular exercises together, and exercises with the US have been cancelled. The Chinese navy uses the port of Sihanoukville as a logistics hub for the frequent stops of its warships, and is planning a naval base in Koh Kong. Cambodia is now forever under Chinese control, and can never wiggle out of China's orbit.

Fifth, yes, the Cambodian government is a puppet regime of China. With China's backing, Cambodia's wily long-serving strongman continues his more-than-three-decades rule. He has basically sold his country to China in exchange for bribes and support of his regime.

China's support has allowed him to turn up his nose at

Western criticism and make Cambodia a family property. When he held the sham national elections of 2018 in which his party of course "won" 100% of the seats in parliament, China mobilized its hackers in widespread cyber activities against his political opponents with the aim of getting information on any opposition activities that threatened his administration. U.S. cybersecurity company FireEye said that given the technology, infrastructure and other factors used, there was no doubt that China was behind the cyber attacks.

He has not only weakened any opposition, but crippled it by using the courts, which are totally corrupt and subservient to him, to charge any major opponents with treason. He has outlawed the main opposition party to make Cambodia effectively a one-party state, cleared the way for himself to be in charge for life, chased out Western NGOs, closed down opposing media outlets via his lackey tax henchmen, and instituted a climate of silent terror where the populace doesn't dare mounting any challenge.

This ruler, his family, and his cronies are in complete control of the country. He has his own thousands-strong bodyguard force, he put a relative at the head of the police, and he elevated his son to be the head of the armed forces with the aim of establishing a dynasty. Whenever the West threatens or implements sanctions, China steps up to his defense and provides political backing and financial relief. With China's urging and backing, the Cambodian leader has turned a deaf ear to the West, and made Cambodia a China protectorate and colony. His party, the CPP, which stands for Cambodian People's Party, might as well be called the Chinese Puppet Party.

China has effectively put a stranglehold on Cambodia, and turned it into a puppet regime that it plays at will on the international scene. For example, China uses Cambodia to stymie any ASEAN efforts to resist its aggressive acts in the South China Sea. China has also gotten Cambodia to significantly downgrade its ties with the US, such as by cancelling joint military exercises with the US, and asking a US Navy aid unit to leave the country.

What a price Cambodia has paid! And all this to the Chinese who regard Cambodians as being lazy and not so bright, and look down on them for being dark-skinned, sometimes even calling them *monkeys*.

So, this is the sorry state of today's Cambodia. Before the Chinese came in droves and took over Cambodia, the French, Americans, Japanese, and other Western countries did help Cambodia after its independence with some financial aid and by building schools, clinics, roads, bridges, water treatment facilities and so on, while also nudging the country toward better governance and more respect for human rights. And these countries did respect Cambodia and its culture. They didn't buy up the country. They didn't trample the local culture. And they didn't destroy the environment. Not so, the Chinese. These Han are truly Huns. Whenever they descend on a place, they come in swarms, take over, and ruin the local culture and environment.

The beautiful country of Cambodia, also known as Kampuchea, which Westerners used to know and flock to, is no more. Cambodia now might as well be called *Kampuchina*. This country's takeover and transformation by the Chinese into a quasi-colony is a stark reminder of the Chinese menace around the world when left unchecked.

6

MILITARY

The armed forces of China are called the People's Liberation Army (PLA). From humble beginnings about a century ago as a guerilla force during the Chinese Civil War, the PLA has been transformed into not only the leading regional power, but also a rising global power that will soon be second to none.

The PLA is very unique among major powers not only in the fact of its meteoric rise, but also in the fact that it's the armed forces of a party, the Communist Party of China (CPC). Indeed, the PLA is under the command of the Central Military Commission (CMC), a commission that is chaired by the general secretary or paramount leader of the CPC.

And the CPC ensures that the military continues to serve it by having political commissars in all the military services and branches. One example to illustrate the PLA's subservience to the CPC is that in 2017, during an inspection of the PLA, paramount leader Xi said, "It must be ensured that the PLA resolutely follows the command of the CPC Central Committee and the CMC at any time, in any circumstances."

The PLA's might has risen in tandem with China's economic development as part of former paramount leader Deng Xiaoping's Four Modernizations initiative, an initiative which targeted the four fields of agriculture, industry, national defense, and science and technology. Ever since Deng Xiaoping's reform and opening-up policy, the PLA has undergone major changes to transform it into a potent modern army that represents the new mighty China. However, during the first two decades of China's reform, most of the country's focus was on economic development, and it was only at the dawn of this twenty-first century that the PLA started its meteoric rise.

China's defense budget in recent years has been second only to that of the US, and dwarfs the defense budgets of neighboring powers Japan, India and Russia. Such abundance of funds combined with the CPC's goal of returning China to its previous world preeminence has enabled the PLA to embark on an unprecedented modernization drive. In a relatively short period of merely a couple of decades, China has become a global power.

China's ultimate goal can be seen in paramount leader Xi's "China Dream," a goal to make China great again, a goal to make China a military superpower that can project its power and enforce its interests around the world. China has already shown its true intentions through aggressive military actions in recent years. It has been building up a formidable arsenal of lethal high-tech weaponry. It has been bullying its weak neighbors in Southeast Asia, and encroaching on their territories or outright occupying them. It has been challenging Japan's territorial integrity on a constant basis. It has been conducting war maneuvers near and around Taiwan. It has been building up logistics and military facilities overseas. And most telling of its

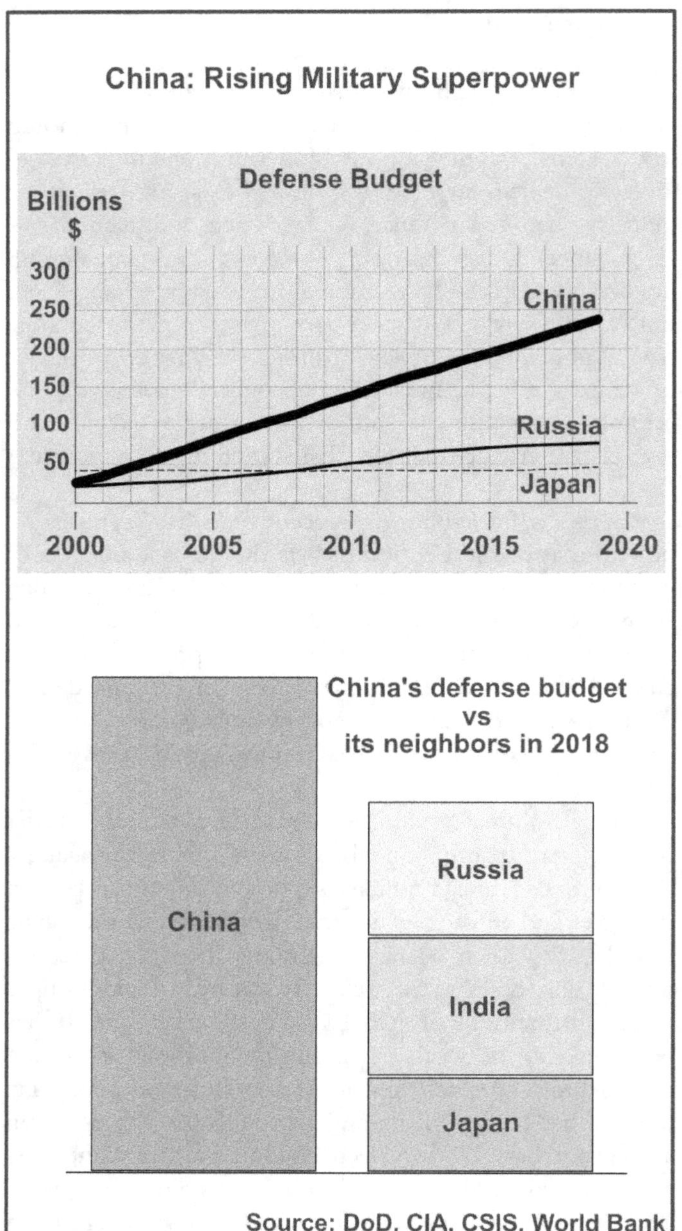
China: Rising Military Superpower
Defense Budget
Billions $
300
250
200
150
100
50
China
Russia
Japan
2000
2005
2010
2015
2020
China's defense budget
vs
its neighbors in 2018
China
Russia
India
Japan
Source: DoD, CIA, CSIS, World Bank

ambitions is that it has been taking on the US head-on in many encounters, whether in the air or in the sea.

China modernizing its armed forces

The PLA's role has evolved since the founding of the People's Republic of China in 1949. Up until the end of the last century, the PLA was mainly a defensive force focused on defending the country's security and territorial integrity although there were exceptions such as during the invasion and occupation of Tibet, the Korean War, the Sino-Indian war, and the Sino-Vietnamese conflict. However, this century as China developed both economically and militarily, the PLA's mission has radically changed.

The PLA's new strategy is to develop into a dominant global military superpower, a status reflective of China's economic might and newfound confidence. China wants to build a military that can take on the US and win, a goal that may happen a lot sooner than what most Western pundits think.

China's strategy for global military preeminence consists of two main stages: regional dominance in the first stage, and global supremacy in the second stage. The first stage is well under way as China has surpassed its main regional adversaries Japan and India, and is rapidly overtaking Russia. In this first stage, China's goal is to protect its ever-expanding core of vital interests. These interests include protecting its territorial integrity, strictly controlling access to its maritime exclusive economic zones, keeping Taiwan under a constant threat of military invasion, enforcing its claims in the East China Sea and South China Sea, and protecting its sea lines of communication.

As for the second stage, China wants to become the dominant world military and eclipse the US by the middle of this century at the very latest. In this stage, China's objectives include taking over Taiwan by military force, and projecting its military might to every corner of the world.

In order to realize its objectives, China has been pulling out all the stops, including spending enormous amounts of money on the modernization of the PLA. Such outlays are huge by any measure, whether using China's own figures or Western estimates. According to official Chinese estimates, China's defense budget in 2019 is $178 billion. However, due to the fact that the Chinese government isn't transparent about its expenditures and may deliberately underestimate the defense budget, and the fact that the government may not have a handle on its own accounting practices, it's widely speculated in the West that China's annual defense budget is way more than $200 billion.

Knowing that the major challenger to its short-tem and long-term goals is the US, China has engaged in an all-out undeclared war against the US, with the intended purpose of first, supplanting the US as the leading power in the Western Pacific, and second, taking the challenge to the US all around the world. Knowing one's enemy well is critical in any war, and China has done its homework on the US. China has learned a lot about the US, its strengths and its weaknesses, and has tailored its efforts accordingly.

China knows that it still can't fully take on the US, and so, as its former paramount leader Deng Xiaoping famously said, it's been biding its time by playing a waiting game and suckering the US into playing along. China has succeeded in lulling the US into believing in its peaceful rise while building up its military.

While biding its time, China has studied the US military and learned a lot about its structure, secrets, and modus operandi. China has also been helped by the fact that the US has been so naïve as to have frequent military exchanges with China and include China in some of its overseas military exercises. Such acquired knowledge of the US military has been invaluable to China. It has helped China realize how its military organization and practices, ones reminiscent of the Soviet model, were so archaic and outdated by modern standards. China came to realize that its military had become very unwieldy and ineffective because of a bloated bureaucracy with many entrenched interests.

Radically restructuring and modernizing the PLA wasn't an easy task until the ascendance to power of the present paramount leader Xi. Xi is a Red Princeling who has risen to a power status not seen since the days of Mao and Deng, and who has shown the gravitas necessary to initiate and implement the radical restructuring of the PLA. Xi's plan is to restructure the PLA in a fundamental way that borrows heavily from the US military. This emulation of the US comes as no surprise given China's track record of copying the US in so many other areas. China is also following the American military model because it's one that has proven its effectiveness in the many wars and conflicts that the US has been engaged in. Xi's plan is to give China a military that's representative of its economic superpower status and that's a representative of the China dream of rejuvenation. Xi's goal is to finish this radical restructuring of the PLA by 2020.

The restructuring that has already taken place or is being implemented includes the following main elements. First, China has been re-divided into five new military regions, called theater commands or battle zones. This reduction in the number of military regions continues a trend that was started many years ago to enhance combat effectiveness.

Second, instead of the old system that was dominated by the ground force or army, the new restructuring gives more emphasis to the navy and air force. In addition, a new force called the Strategic Support Force was created.

Third, a joint services command has been created. This is a total revamping of the structure and modus operandi of the PLA, and is based on the US model of military operations.

Fourth, the size of the PLA, whose personnel at 2.3 million is the world's largest, is being trimmed to two million to make it leaner and more efficient. Most of the cuts come from the army, which had grown into a bloated, bureaucratic, unwieldy entity.

And fifth, the chain of command among the different services and branches has been clarified and streamlined. Thus, operational commands follow a three-tier process from the CMC to the theater commands, and then from the theater commands to the troops. As for the administrative commands, they flow from the CMC to the headquarters of the different services, and then from the headquarters to their respective services.

The newly restructured PLA consists of the following five branches: Army, Navy, Air Force, Rocket Force, and Strategic Support Force. In addition to these branches, the PLA is supported by the People's Armed Police and the People's Liberation Army militia.

The Army used to be the dominant service in the PLA

China's Military Organization

Theater Commands (TC's)

NORTHERN
SY
BJ
WESTERN
CENTRAL
NJ
CD
EASTERN
BJ: Beijing
CD: Chengdu
GZ: Guangzhou
NJ: Nanjing
SY: Shenyang
SOUTHERN
GZ

Military Chain of Command

CMC

PLA Army HQ
PLA Navy HQ
TC's
PLA Strategic Support Force
PLA Air Force HQ
PLA Rocket Force HQ

Ground Forces
Naval Forces
Air Forces
Missile Forces

Source: DoD

in both the number of personnel and the level of importance. Its headquarters were the general headquarters of the whole PLA. However, under the latest reorganization of the PLA, the Army has gone through two major changes. First, as part of leveling the status of the services, the Army is now considered a service on par with others like the Navy and Air Force, and has been assigned its own service headquarters, again just like the Navy and the Air Force. Second, the Army has born the brunt of the reductions in personnel that are part of the restructuring of the PLA. Xinhua reported in 2019 that the army now accounts for less than 50% of the total number of PLA troops. The logic is that China doesn't expect any major conflicts on its land borders, and needs to spend more resources on other services like the Navy and Air Force.

Besides this latest reorganization, the Army has been going through a mechanization and "informatization" process to modernize it and make it more effective so as to be able to engage in multiple simultaneous land wars. Thus, it has acquired all types of new equipment, such as tanks, armored personnel carriers, artillery, and helicopters.

In contrast to the reduced importance given to the Army, the Navy has been receiving increased attention and funding. A strong navy is essential to China's survival as it's needed to protect the country's sea lines of communication, and equally important to deal with China's natural naval problem of being encircled by chains of islands that the US and regional powers can use to blockade China. China depends heavily on maritime trade and such a blockade would lead to the collapse of the Chinese economy.

China has over a relatively short period of time emerged as a maritime superpower. Its coastguard now has

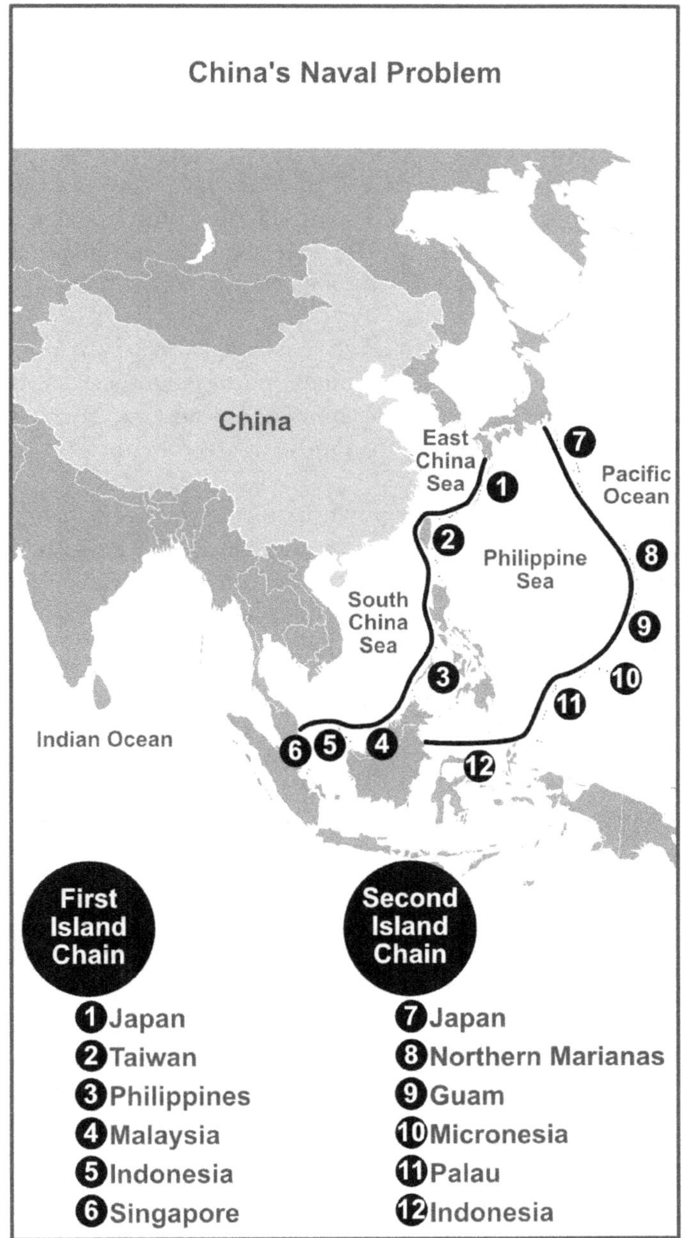
China's Naval Problem
China
East China Sea
Pacific Ocean
Philippine Sea
South China Sea
Indian Ocean
1
2
3
4
5
6
7
8
9
10
11
12
First Island Chain
1 Japan
2 Taiwan
3 Philippines
4 Malaysia
5 Indonesia
6 Singapore
Second Island Chain
7 Japan
8 Northern Marianas
9 Guam
10 Micronesia
11 Palau
12 Indonesia

the world's largest fleet. Its fishing armada, which doubles as a maritime militia, numbers some 200,000 seagoing vessels. And its navy is now bigger than the US Navy in terms of number of vessels. Indeed, according to the New York Times, in 2017 China's Navy overtook the US as the world's largest navy with 317 surface vessels and subs in active service while the US had 283. Not only has China surpassed the US, but it's also increasing the quantity and quality of its vessels at a stunning and unmatched rate.

China has also invested in a vast network of harbors around the world, and the Chinese port operators are now the world leaders. Chinese shipping companies, such as Cosco, carry more cargo than those of any other nation.

China's Navy has outgrown its former role as a mainly coastal force to develop into a true blue-water navy. It is organized into three major fleets: the North Sea Fleet based in Qingdao, the East Sea Fleet based in Ningbo, and the South Sea Fleet based in Zhenjiang.

The modernization of the Navy has seen legacy ships and weapons been phased out and replaced with more capable modern ones. The Navy's inventory includes aircraft carriers, submarines, destroyers, frigates, corvettes, amphibious ships, and supply ships.

The surface-ships fleet now includes an aircraft carrier, and a second rather similar one should be operational by 2020. The ski-ramp design of these two flattops places limitations on the types of aircraft that can be launched and on the aircraft's armament payload. The first aircraft carrier is playing an important role in training China's squads of present and future naval aviators, and has been deployed in China's near seas, that is the East China Sea and South China Sea. The second flattop will likely be deployed to the Indian Ocean to protect China's sea lines

China: Rise of a Maritime Leviathan
World Rank
China Navy fleet size: 1
China Coast Guard fleet size: 1
China's fishing armada fleet size: 1
Chinese port operators: 1
Source: DoD, FT

of communication.

These two aircraft carriers are just the beginning as most observers agree that China will expand this fleet of two flattops to four or six, with carrier strike groups initially based in the Western Pacific and the Indian Ocean. The future Chinese flattops are expected to be just as big as US carriers, will use some type of catapult system similar to that of US carriers, and may be nuclear-powered.

In addition to the aircraft carriers, the surface-ships fleet includes powerful guided-missile destroyers and frigates that are equipped with advanced anti-ship and anti-air weapons and sensors. They can launch anti-ship cruise missiles, land-attack cruise missiles, antisubmarine missiles, and surface-to-air missiles. For example, China's latest destroyer, the type 055 guided-missile destroyer, can fire HHQ-9 surface-to-air missiles, YJ-18 anti-ship cruise missiles, CJ-10 land-attack cruise missiles and missile-launched anti-submarine torpedoes. This destroyer, big enough to be classified as a cruiser, sports advanced features such as an advanced X-band radar in four active electronically scanned arrays and an integrated electronic system similar to the Aegis combat system on US naval ships.

The surface-ships fleet also includes a large number of corvettes that are ideally suited to serve China's interests in the East China Sea and South China Sea, and a number of amphibious ships that give China an expeditionary capability. These amphibious ships can carry landing craft, helicopters, armored vehicles, and troops.

Besides the surface ships, a large and expanding fleet of nuclear-powered and diesel-powered submarines lurk in China's territorial waters and roam the world's oceans. This fleet includes not only attack submarines, but also a handful of nuclear ballistic missile submarines. The attack submarines can launch anti-ship cruise missiles and soon land-attack cruise missiles too. The nuclear ballistic missile submarines give China a potent sea-based nuclear deterrent.

China is also developing autonomous robotic submarines, called Unmanned Underwater Vehicles (UUVs), that can roam the world's oceans to perform a wide range of missions, from reconnaissance to mine placement and even suicide attacks against enemy vessels. These low-cost AI subs can even take down multi-billion-dollar US nuclear subs.

In addition to ships, the Navy also operates various types of naval aircraft to provide fleet defense, support amphibious operations, engage in anti-submarine and anti-ship warfare, and patrol and defend the coastline and territorial waters. One aircraft of worthy note is the aircraft-carrier-based fighter, the J-15, also known as the *Flying Shark*, which is based on Russia's Sukhoi Su-33 fighter, a prototype of which China bought from the Ukraine and then reverse engineered. The J-15 is reported to be equipped with advanced avionics providing multi-target capability and resistance to jamming. It can carry various types of armaments including supersonic anti-ship missiles.

The J-15 has performance and stability problems in addition to being too heavy. It's based on stolen Russian technology that's too old and that was actually intended for a land-based fighter. In fact, so many J-15s have crashed and burned that Chinese media came to refer to the jet as a "flopping fish." Thus, China is developing the J-31, a fifth-generation fighter based on stolen US technology, to replace the aging J-15.

Finally, underlying China's plans to project its naval power to the far seas and oceans and to protect its sea lines of communication, the Marine Corps is in the process of a massive build-out that will boost its size by about 400% to 100,000. Many of these marines are to be deployed overseas, such as to the new Chinese naval base in Djibouti and the Chinese-operated port of Gwadar in Pakistan.

Just as China's Navy has made great strides in its modernization drive, so too has the Air Force. China's Air Force, which used to be a short-range defensive force focused on defending the mainland and coastal areas, has been greatly transformed into a modern and multi-role force capable of not only projecting China's power far beyond its borders, but also challenging the US.

China's Air Force has reduced its huge inventory of legacy combat and support aircraft, and replaced them with modern aircraft. Thus, fourth-generation fighters now make up half of the force. These fighters are quite capable; for example, the J-10 and J-11 fighters are equivalent in capability to the upgraded US F-15.

The history behind these two Chinese fighter jets is quite interesting. The J-10 looks like the US F-16, and for good reason. Indeed, China used F-16 technologies that it secretly bought from Israel in the 1980s and 1990s to develop its J-10. Over the years, China kept upgrading the J-10 and now it sports enhancements such as an advanced fire control radar array and composite materials. As for the J-11, it's based on Russia's Sukhoi Su-27, whose production China licensed from the collapsing Soviet Union in 1989.

2017 saw the official debut of the J-16 fighter jet, which is based on Russia's Sukhoi-30 fighter jet. The J-16, described as a 4.5-generation fighter jet, is a long-range, twin-engine, tandem-seat, multirole, all-weather fighter jet with advanced avionics for electronic warfare and comes equipped with air-to-air missiles, satellite-guided smart bombs, and anti-ship missiles. China is also developing an electronic attack version, the J-16D. This jet will be equivalent to the US EA-18G Growler, and is to serve as an advanced airborne electronic attack platform.

China is also in the process of fielding fifth-generation fighters, the J-20 and J-31, which are supposed to rival the US Air Force's F-22 Raptor and F-35 Joint Strike Fighter. According to experts, the two Chinese planes borrow heavily from their US counterparts. In fact, the classified plans for the US jets were stolen by a Chinese national named Su Bin, who was arrested and sent to prison in the US.

The difference between these two fifth-generation jets is that the J-20 is the more capable plane, whereas the J-31 is geared for exports to other countries. Although it's not as stealthy as the US jets and can't match them as a dogfighter, the J-20 is designed as a high-speed, long-range interceptor that carries a heavy payload of long-range air-to-air missiles. Instead of taking on the US jets head-to-head in air battles, the J-20 can hit the US at a soft point by going after the airborne support planes, the AWACS and the refueling tankers, from a safe distance and thereby severely reducing the reach of US attack aircraft and severely crippling the US ability to conduct long-range sustained air campaigns.

In addition to its indigenous fighters, China has a fleet of Russian fighters like the Su-27, the Su-30, and the modern and potent Su-35.

Besides fighter jets, China's Air Force has also been

actively upgrading support aircraft, such as AWACS (Airborne Warning And Control Systems) airplanes, refueling tankers, and heavy-lift cargo planes in order to project its power on a regional basis and later globally. This air strategy of projecting power is similar to the naval strategy of deploying aircraft carriers.

As part of this strategy, existing bombers have been retrofitted for long-range missions, and a new long-range stealth bomber is already under development. China's current strategic bomber, the H-6 built by Xi'an Aviation, is a knockoff of the 1950s-era Soviet Tu-16 Badger. The H-6 bomber has been upgraded with modern avionics, aerial refueling capability and cruise missiles in the later H-6K and H-6J models.

China's next generation strategic bomber is the H-20, also built by Xi'an Aviation. It's a stealthy flying wing like the US B-2 with a maximum unrefueled combat radius exceeding 5,000 miles and payload of more than ten tons. This long-range capability will allow the H-20 to strike targets as far as Hawaii. The H-20 will also be able to carry nuclear weapons, cementing China's nuclear deterrence triad of nuclear-capable submarines, land-based ballistic missiles, and bombers.

China's quick rise in the aircraft field is mainly due to its blatant copying of Russian designs and stealing of US secrets. One critical piece of aircraft design that China hasn't been able to master so far is that of jet engines. China has relied on importing such engines from Russia. However, due to Russia's hesitance to keep supplying engines to China, an understandable reaction by Russia since China keeps blatantly ripping off Russian designs, and also due to China's realization that it needs to wean itself from Russian dependence, China in 2016 formed a huge state-owned company, Aero Engine Corporation of

China, to lead the country's efforts in the research, development and manufacture of aircraft engines for China's aviation industry.

In addition to manned aircraft, China has become a leader in the UAV (unmanned aerial vehicle) field. Various such drones have been developed and deployed. They come in various sizes, from the hand-launched to the taxiing models, and can be used for a variety of missions. These missions could be for a support role, such as for reconnaissance, surveillance, target-acquisition, and communications, or for attack by carrying a variety of weapons, such as laser-guided missiles and bombs. Drones are well suited for these missions because of their low cost, inherent or built-in stealth, long endurance, and long loitering time at various altitudes. China is even working on fielding swarms of drones that would operate autonomously and overwhelm an enemy.

Worthy of note is the Chinese drone CH-5, a direct competitor of the US Reaper. The CH-5 can be used for reconnaissance, early warning, and attack missions. It can carry up to 16 air-to-ground missiles and stay in the air for two days, or even five days with some modifications. Such endurance allows it to cover up to 10,000km.

Finally, the Chinese Air Force has been equipped with very-long-range air-to-air missiles with twice the range of US missiles, and with hypersonic speeds much higher than those of US missiles. Such missiles serve Chinese fighters well in case of a conflict with the US. In such a conflict, the Chinese fighters would not need to go head to head against superior US fighters, but could rather go after US support aircraft, such as the AWACS and tankers, from safe long distances.

Besides the Army, Navy and Air Force, the other

traditional PLA service is the Rocket Force, which is the main missile division of the PLA, and which is in charge of the land-based nuclear and conventional missiles. China's missiles have become a potent force as China has not only fielded huge numbers of them, but also improved their range, accuracy, and survivability.

The Rocket Force's arsenal includes hundreds of ballistic and cruise missiles. These missiles can be used to attack both land targets and moving surface ships, such as aircraft carriers. Short-range missiles can hit targets all over Taiwan. Medium and intermediate-range missiles can strike targets in the first island chain, such as the US bases in Japan, and targets in the second island chain, such as Guam.

One deadly cruise missile is the CJ-10, which has a range of 1,500 km, can be armed with a conventional or nuclear payload, and can be launched from land, sea, and air. It flies at low altitude to evade radar detection, and is equipped with a navigation system that uses inertial navigation, satellite navigation, and terrain matching. Adding to its lethality is the fact that it can be re-targeted in mid-flight.

The anti-ship ballistic missiles (ASBMs) could be game-changers in modern naval warfare. These Chinese ASBMs have been developed with the principal aim of sinking enemy, i.e. US, aircraft carriers, and are reported to be indefensible because of their maneuverability in finding and homing in on targets. China is also working on making these missiles hypersonic, thus making them even more potent. This strategy of attacking ships via land-based missiles has been so impactful that the Pentagon has decided to follow suit and develop such a capability too.

China's Intercontinental Nuclear Ballistic Missiles

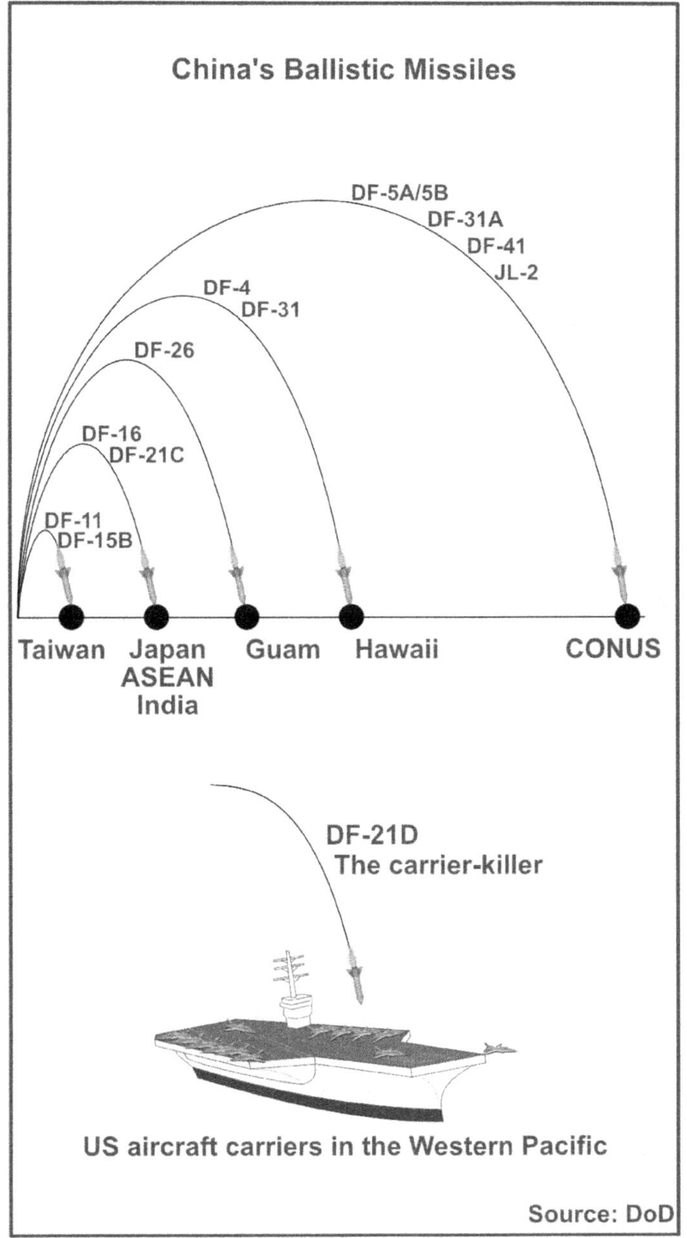
China's Ballistic Missiles
DF-5A/5B
DF-31A
DF-41
JL-2
DF-4
DF-31
DF-26
DF-16
DF-21C
DF-11
DF-15B
Taiwan
Japan
ASEAN
India
Guam
Hawaii
CONUS
DF-21D
The carrier-killer
US aircraft carriers in the Western Pacific
Source: DoD

(ICBMs) can reach all targets in the US. In addition to the silo-based missiles, China has been fielding more survivable mobile-delivery systems. According to some reports, China has built tunnel networks that stretch for thousands of miles underground to hide its mobile missiles.

China's latest ICBM, the DF-41, is road-mobile, has the longest range of any nuclear missile in the world, and can carry up to a dozen nuclear warheads.

In addition to the aforementioned four services and as part of the new reorganization of the PLA, China has created the Strategic Support Force, a force that will integrate all the information systems and tasks that are necessary to win "informatized" or "informationized" wars. This force is to support the PLA's joint combat operations in the domains of space warfare, electromagnetic warfare, and cyber warfare. This force includes the military's espionage branch, the group responsible for electronic spying and cyber attacks.

This force's consolidation of the management of information assets and information flow will significantly boost the PLA's combat effectiveness. And in order to accomplish its mission, this force can count on an impressive arsenal of assets. For example, in the space domain, China not only has its own global satellite navigation system, but it also has tens of military satellites that are used for communications, navigation, weather forecasting, warning, and spying. And to counter the US military satellite system, China has at its disposal many anti-satellite capabilities, such as laser weapons, jammers, satellite-killer missiles that can reach geosynchronous orbits, and dual-use space technology.

Major Global Satellite Navigation Systems

Name	Owner	Status	Number of Satellites
GPS	US	Fully operational	32
GLONASS	Russia	Fully operational	26
Galileo	EU	Fully operational by 2020	30
Beidou	China	Fully operational by 2020	35

Source: China Satellite Navigation Office, GPS.gov

China's military expansionism

Gone are the days when China was reticent to refer to its *rise*. And gone are the days when China strictly followed the line of its former paramount leader Deng Xiaoping to "hide its strength and bide its time." These are the days of China's gung-ho jingoism and truculent diplomacy. These are the days when China has finally revealed its hidden agenda, that of using force to regain its past glory and to redress what it deems as past injustices against it by the West and other powers.

Given that most of China's land-border disputes have either been settled to China's advantage or gone into extended hibernation to China's satisfaction, the new belligerent China has turned its focus to its maritime claims, which are outrageously expansive, and to projecting its military power around the world. Thus, China has laid claims to most of the East China Sea and South China Sea, and is actively stamping its hegemony over those international water bodies and surrounding countries. China has also been building up its power in the Western Pacific, cementing its status as a permanent power in the Indian Ocean, and establishing overseas bases as far away as Africa. China even has designs on the Arctic Ocean as it now calls itself a "Near-Arctic" nation, to the consternation of the US.

In the East China Sea, China has over the last decade ramped up its dispute with Japan over the Senkaku Islands, which China calls Diaoyu Islands, and over the demarcation of their respective exclusive economic zones in that sea. China has been aggressively pushing its claims.

With regards to the Senkaku Islands, China has been constantly violating Japan's sovereignty over those islands and surrounding territorial waters with regular incursions

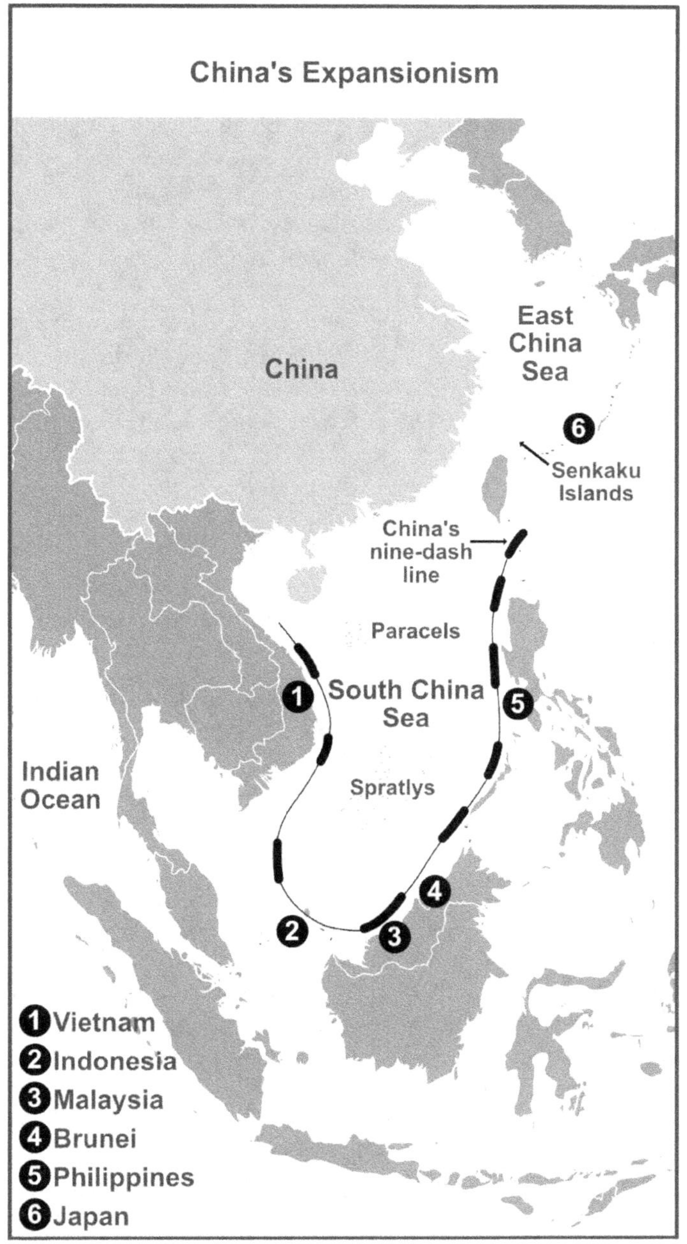
China's Expansionism
China
East
China
Sea
Senkaku
Islands
China's
nine-dash
line
Paracels
South China
Sea
Indian
Ocean
Spratlys
Vietnam
Indonesia
Malaysia
Brunei
Philippines
Japan

by its coast guard, navy, and militia ships. Chinese fishing trawlers always try to sneak in and illegally fish in those waters. China encourages jingoistic citizens to sail boats to those islands, land on them, and plant China's flag, thus forcing Japan time and again to remove them and send them back. And China's military aircraft regularly violate Japan's air space near those islands, forcing Japan to be on constant alert and to scramble fighter jets in response.

And with respect to the maritime demarcation between Japan and China in the East China Sea, China is drilling for gas in areas of that sea that are claimed by Japan. China has also declared an air defense identification zone over much of the East China Sea. And China has gone so far as to suggest that Okinawa and the Ryukyu Islands do not belong to Japan.

While in the East China Sea, Japan is no pushover and has so far resolutely stood up to China's challenge, in the South China Sea China has had its way with its weak Southeast Asian neighbors and is well on its way to controlling most of that sea, all while the US keeps dithering about any type of firm response and keeps practicing paper-tiger freedom-of-navigation maneuvers that do nothing but reaffirm China's domination of the area.

China claims most of the South China Sea, a claim famously referred to as the "nine-dash line." This claim is so outrageous that it has no precedent in the annals of modern history. China is claiming international waters that are more than a thousand miles away from its mainland coast. It's claiming everything that's inside the South China Sea, including islands, islets, reefs, cays, atolls, shoals, and fishing waters. Not only that, but China's nine-dash line butts right up to the coasts of bordering countries, disregarding those countries' legal right to their exclusive economic zones. China's claim can only be described as utterly ridiculous. However, China, as a rising belligerent superpower, sees its claim as logical for as its top diplomat and former foreign minister, Yang Jiechi, once said, "China is a big country and other countries are small countries, and that is just a fact."

China's bid to enforce its claim over the South China Sea has gone through three phases. The first phase saw China bullying its nearest neighbor in the South China Sea, Vietnam, and taking over its possessions in that sea. Thus, back in the 1950s when Vietnam was divided and weak, China got North Vietnam to cede the Paracel Islands to it. And in 1974, when South Vietnam tried to reclaim the islands, China routed the South Vietnamese from the islands and took complete control of the Paracels. It's interesting to note that at that time South Vietnam requested the help of its American ally, but the US declined and the US Seventh Fleet stayed away from that conflict, a pattern that disturbingly happened later with other allies, and a pattern that was rightly mocked by the Philippines president Duterte when he announced his rapprochement with China. And China wasn't done with Vietnam after the latter reunified into one country and restated its sovereignty demands over the Paracels and Spratlys. In 1988, after a brief land war and about a decade of skirmishes, China routed the Vietnamese navy in the Spratly Islands and took over six reefs: Cuarteron Reef, Hughes Reef, Fiery Cross Reef, Gaven Reefs, Johnson South Reef, and Subi Reef. And in 1995, China occupied Mischief Reef, to the consternations of not only Vietnam, but also the Philippines.

The second phase took place in this century, especially the second decade, as China became an economic superpower and the leading regional military with a formidable Navy, Coast Guard, Air Force, and Rocket

Force. In this second phase, China became overly aggressive in enforcing its claim over the South China Sea, not only vis-à-vis its weak Southeast Asian neighbors but also towards other powers that dared to challenge it, notably the US.

Thus, in 2009, Chinese ships harassed the US surveillance ship USNS Impeccable while it was conducting routine operations in international waters by maneuvering dangerously close to it, ordering it to leave the area, and trying to rip off its towed sonar array. Also in 2009, a Chinese submarine rammed and damaged a sonar array towed by the USS John S. McCain destroyer near Subic Bay off the coast of the Philippines. In 2011, Chinese ships harassed a Vietnamese oil and gas survey ship and cut its cables while it was in Vietnam's territorial waters off its south-central coast. In 2012, China took over sole control of Scarborough Shoal, reneging on a deal brokered by the paper-tiger Obama administration. In 2014, a Chinese ship rammed and sank a Vietnamese boat during a confrontation between the two countries when China forcibly set up an oil rig in an area claimed by Vietnam. In 2014, China began turning Mischief Reef and others into artificial islands. In 2015, a China Coast Guard vessel illegally anchored in Luconia Shoals and claimed sovereignty over them even though they belong to and lie very close to Malaysia. In 2016, Chinese J-11 fighter jets intercepted a US Navy reconnaissance aircraft flying in international airspace over the South China Sea. And in July 2016, when the Permanent Court of Arbitration ruled that China's nine-dash-line claim to the South China Sea had no legal basis, China immediately rejected the ruling as null and void.

It's worth noting that China's most egregious acts of belligerence occurred during the Obama administration whose dovish diplomacy greatly hampered the US military and let China get away with murder. The Chinese leaders saw Obama as weak, and took full advantage. As noted Indonesian Dr. Anwar once remarked, "China respects strength. If they see you as being weak, they'll eat you alive." The Chinese treated Obama with contempt and as a culminating act of disrespect toward him in the final days of his presidency, in December 2016 a Chinese navy ship stole an American underwater research drone in full view of a US crew. This was a premeditated act as the Chinese ship had been shadowing the US ship, which deployed the drone. This was a grave in-your-face act, maybe even an act of war, and showed the total disrespect that the Chinese had for the Obama administration. And the Chinese were completely right in their assessment of Obama. While the Chinese stole the US drone and kept it for days during which they analyzed its secrets, all that Obama did was to issue a demarche, a formal diplomatic protest, to ask for its return.

Obama's strategy toward China was laughable. This is a guy who, while the Chinese were basically spitting in his face, declared, "I've been very explicit in saying that we have more to fear from a weakened, threatened China than a successful, rising China." Such thinking is the problem of moronic American leaders living in a fantasy world where they think they enhance their political cred and legacy by engaging in highfaluting take-the-high-road pronouncements espousing the notion of engaging China in a win-win modus vivendi, while the Chinese live in the down-and-dirty take-no-prisoners real world of winning at all costs.

During this second phase of China's bid to take over the South China Sea, China built up its military in that sea in total ignorance of the US and others' lame objections. In the Paracel Islands, China deployed surface-to-air missiles and anti-ship cruise missiles on Woody Island. In the Spratly Islands, over a period of just two years from 2014 to 2016, China went on a construction frenzy and reclaimed more than 3,000 acres to build up its reefs into artificial islands with ports big enough to accommodate its warships and runways long enough to land any of its military aircraft. By comparison, the other South China Sea claimants, Vietnam, the Philippines, Malaysia and Taiwan, reclaimed a total of only about 45 acres over four decades! China also erected military support facilities, such as radar stations, hangars for fighter jets and other military aircraft, and shelters for mobile missile launchers.

The third phase of China's bid to take full control of the South China Sea is now underway and will see China establishing a de-facto control over that sea by the activation of its newly built military bases. In this phase, China can be expected to deploy personnel, civilian and military, to make the bases fully operational. China will gradually but surely deploy troops and armament, including fighter jets, destroyers, submarines, missiles and anti-missile defense systems. According to US intelligence sources quoted by CNBC in 2018, China has already installed anti-ship cruise missiles (YJ-12B with a range of 295 nautical miles) and long-range surface-to-air missile systems (HQ-9B with a range of 160 nautical miles) in the Spratlys, giving it the ability to shoot down or sink enemy aircraft and naval ships. China can also be expected to declare an air defense identification zone over the whole airspace of the South China Sea, and enforce a fishing permit rule. And China will seek to fully integrate its South China Sea outposts with the mainland via regular cruises just as it has already done with the Paracel Islands.

The East China Sea and South China Sea are but a steppingstone for China's global ambitions as evidenced by the surge in Chinese military activities around the world, such as Chinese navy ships patrolling near the US West

Coast or conducting joint maneuvers with the Russian navy in the Mediterranean. China's rationale for the buildup and worldwide projection of its military is that it needs to protect its sea lines of communication and interests around the world. While this is a valid argument, the fact is that China has ulterior motives too, those of challenging the US global supremacy and ultimately stamping its hegemony over the world.

A telling illustration of China's global military ambitions is its "String of Pearls," a series of Chinese naval bases and logistics hubs that stretch from the South China Sea to the Indian Ocean, and all the way to Africa. From east to west, these Chinese outposts include the aforementioned Paracels and Spratleys in the South China Sea, Sihanoukville and Koh Kong in Cambodia, Kyaukpyu and the Coco Islands in Myanmar, Chittagong in Bangladesh, Hambantota in Sri Lanka, Gwadar in Pakistan, Djibouti, and Lamu in Kenya.

These naval bases and logistics hubs are the result of China's economic and military expansionism. Thus, when it comes to the Chinese takeover of ports in Cambodia, the fact is that Cambodia has become a China satellite. China is Cambodia's economic and military master. In the economy, the Chinese and the Chinese Khmers have a stranglehold on the Cambodian economy, and in the military, China trains the Cambodian forces and is their main supplier of weapons.

Cambodia has become so beholden to China that it does China's bidding in keeping ASEAN fragmented and ineffective against China in the South China Sea conflict. Cambodia is now basically a Chinese quasi-colony as hundreds of thousands of Chinese have moved to the country and taken over many strategic assets. The Chinese are using the port of Sihanoukville as a logistics hub, and

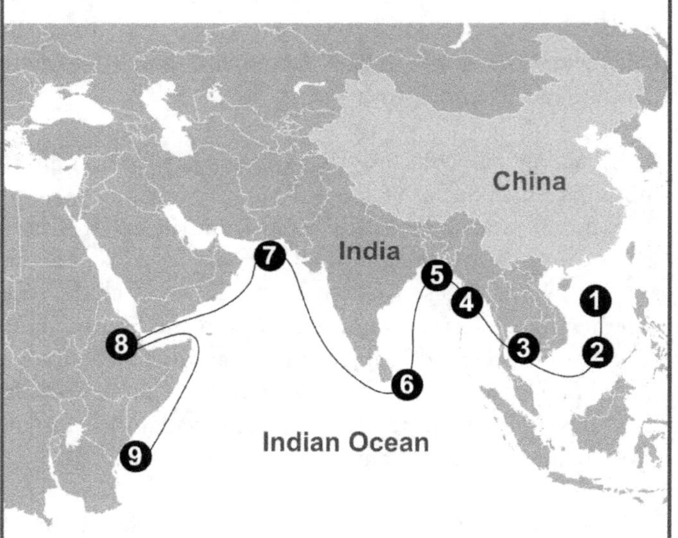

1 Paracel Islands

2 Spratly Islands

3 Cambodia: Sihanoukville, Koh Kong

4 Myanmar: Sittwe, Kyaukpyu, Coco Islands

5 Bangladesh: Chittagong

6 Sri Lanka: Hambantota, Colombo

7 Pakistan: Gwadar

8 Djibouti

9 Kenya: Lamu

are prepping ports in Sihanouk and Koh Kong provinces for naval bases.

Near Cambodia is another country that China has in its pocket and that is Myanmar. China did have a long and close relationship with Myanmar while it was under a military dictatorship. China is suspected of having used that cozy relationship with the Myanmar military to install secret radar stations on the Coco Islands in the Bay of Bengal to keep an eye and spy on India.

Now that Myanmar has ditched its dictatorship and embarked on "democratic" rule, China has upped the ante with major economic investments, especially in the China-Myanmar economic corridor. This corridor from the port of Kyaukpyu in Myanmar to the Chinese city of Kunming is already operational with pipelines pumping Middle Eastern oil and Myanmar natural gas to China. China plans to expand this corridor with highways and railroads. This corridor has great importance to China as it allows it to bypass the Malacca Strait bottleneck for its energy imports.

The port of Kyaukpyu is being developed into a major industrial zone with China holding a majority stake that allows it to control the port. Such control provides China's navy with important logistical support in the Bay of Bengal and Indian Ocean. China has ensured the continuation of its cozy relationship with Myanmar by steadfastly supporting Myanmar's new strongwoman Suu Kyi and her genocide against the Rohingya minority.

Besides Cambodia and Myanmar, another Southeast Asian country, Thailand, has been pulled into China's orbit. Indeed, with the political and economic support of China, the Thai military has turned Thailand's democracy into a joke and now controls the government regardless of any elections. The Thai military holds China's authoritarian type of government as an ideal to emulate, and has been growing closer ties with the Chinese military.

The Chinese have been pouring into Thailand as both tourists and investors. Given that Chinese Thais already dominated the Thai economy, the new influx of Chinese investments can only help China in its quest to dominate Thailand and completely wean it from Western influence. One significant investment that China has been contemplating is building a canal in the south of Thailand, in the Isthmus of Kra. Such a canal would allow China to bypass the chokepoint that is the Malacca Strait and help it secure its sea lines of communication.

China highly values the strategic locations of Thailand and Myanmar on the Andaman Sea and the Bay of Bengal since they offer great vantage points from which China can keep an eye on its South Asian nemesis, India. However, Myanmar and Thailand aren't China's only targets in this region, as China has also been cultivating very close ties with Bangladesh. China is Bangladesh's biggest trading partner and biggest arms supplier. China has sold to Bangladesh all types of weaponry, including tanks, aircraft, corvettes, anti-ship missiles, and even submarines. China has tried to build a deep-water port in Bangladesh, such as in Chittagong, but due to heavy pressure from India, Japan and the US, Bangladesh has hesitated on letting China be the sole builder or operator of a port.

Whatever decision Bangladesh takes with regards to building a deep-water port, China can count on its close ties with that country for at least naval logistical access and support. China has already scored a big win in weaning Bangladesh from India's dominance, and will keep on solidifying its ties with Bangladesh to keep it as a thorn in India's back.

While in the north of the Bay of Bengal, China is still working on establishing a firm toehold in Bangladesh, such is not the case in the south of that bay as China has been able to subjugate the strategically-located island of Sri Lanka. Indeed, using predatory economics to build economically-nonviable major infrastructure that left Sri Lanka heavily indebted to China, the latter has scored a major coup in forcing this Indian Ocean country to hand over the operational management and control of the strategic Hambantota deep-water port to a Chinese company under a lease that will keep this port in Chinese hands for a century. Located on the south coast of Sri Lanka, this port gives China's navy a very important vantage point from which its destroyers and submarines can roam the Indian Ocean on a permanent basis.

China's presence in the Indian Ocean is greatly reinforced by its close relationship with another bordering country, Pakistan. This country and China have what they proudly refer to as an "all-weather friendship."

China has invested heavily in Pakistan, and has committed to investing around $50 billion in the China-Pakistan Economic Corridor. This investment plan will see a major overhaul of the Pakistani infrastructure in roads, rail, communications, and power generation. However, the crown jewel of China's investments in Pakistan is the strategically located deep-water port of Gwadar, which lies next door to the oil states of the Persian Gulf. This port has been rebuilt and expanded by China and is on lease to a Chinese company for at least four decades. China is building a huge industrial park next to the port, and plans to build a mega oil pipeline to ship Middle Eastern oil from Gwadar to Kashgar in China.

China uses Gwadar not only as a special economic zone and naval logistics hub, but also as a future naval base where the Chinese navy can deploy its marines and warships. In 2018, reports surfaced that China was also contemplating the construction of a military base in Jiwani, a port west of Gwadar and close to the Iranian border.

This Chinese military expansion in Pakistan is due to the very close Sino-Pakistani military ties. China is Pakistan's top arms supplier, and has been supplying the country with arms for decades. China was the major force behind the development of Pakistan's nuclear weapons program. Also, the two countries have co-developed military aircraft, and Pakistan has shared US military secrets with China, secrets such as those of the F-15 fighter jet, the tomahawk missile, and the Black Hawk stealth helicopter, which was downed during the raid by US Special Forces to kill Osama Bin Laden in Pakistan.

Another reason that Pakistan wants the Chinese navy in Gwadar and Jiwani is to prevent an Indian blockade in case of a war between the two South Asian countries. Indeed, India would have to think twice before taking on China because China now has deployed assets to encircle India on all sides: in the Bay of Bengal to the west, in Sri Lanka to the south, in Pakistan to the West, and in the Himalayas to the north.

Using these Pakistani ports, which sit practically at the mouth of the Persian Gulf, allows China to safeguard its important energy imports from that gulf's states. Such is the importance of this region to China that the latter has invested heavily in another country at the mouth of the Persian Gulf, Oman. This weak, impoverished and sparsely populated country, whose main export is crude oil that mostly goes to China, suits China's predatory economics quite well, and China will surely exact some concessions in return for its huge investments. The Chinese have their eyes on the strategically located port of Duqm in which they're investing billions of dollars.

China's presence in the Indian Ocean includes not only outposts all along Asia's southern coast, but also outposts in Africa, as Djibouti has become a major Chinese overseas military base. This base is ironically situated just a few miles away from the US naval base of Camp Lemonnier in that same country. This proximity not only allows China to keep an eye on and learn a lot about the US military, but also is very symbolic in showing the world that China has become an equal to the US.

And China's influence in Djibouti is rising and will dwarf that of the US. Indeed, while the US interest in Djibouti is purely as a military base, China has gone all out to win over Djibouti with its soft power. China is investing billions of dollars in Djibouti to expand its port, build new airports, and construct a huge free trade zone to make Djibouti into the gateway for Ethiopia, South Sudan, Somalia, and the Great Lakes region. China has already inaugurated a new railway line that it built from Ethiopia's capital Addis Ababa to Djibouti, and is working on other rail projects. And China has also opened a Confucius Institute in Djibouti to fashion the minds of the young generation of Djiboutians.

Besides Djibouti, China has its eyes on developing other logistics and naval bases in Africa. A prominent such location is the port of Lamu in Kenya, which China is developing into a major port that will be connected via Chinese-built rail to Ethiopia and South Sudan.

The fact is that most of Africa is in China's pocket. China has for decades invested heavily and cultivated close ties with most African countries. China's PLA would be welcomed with open arms and given support at any time in such countries as Algeria, Sudan, Ethiopia, Tanzania,

Namibia and Angola.

China's military expansion is gradually extending to the rest of the world. An eye-opening and ominous example is that China has even established a toehold in Australia. Indeed, in 2015, a Chinese company with links to the PLA leased the port of Darwin for 99 years, and expressed interest in other Australian ports. According to The Guardian, the Darwin deal gives the Chinese company 100% operational control of the port and 80% ownership. This gives the Chinese a vantage point from which to observe the US Marines, who are deployed in that region, and to control the Marines' supply base. Cynics might say that this is a Chinese civilian company, but when it comes to China the civilian and military objectives are tightly intertwined.

China readying for war with the US

The US is presently the dominant global power, and China is the rising power that's challenging America's dominance. In 2018, at the Aspen Security Forum in Colorado, a top CIA expert, Michael Collins, said about the Chinese, "What they're waging against us is fundamentally a cold war." History teaches us that in most of such rivalries, the two powers are bound to go to war. This scenario is even more likely given China's view of the world as a zero-sum game in which it must prevail.

The later this war breaks out, the more the odds are in China's favor. The US is a lumbering giant hampered by partisan bickering among its governing parties and the wasting of valuable resources on ill-advised conflicts around the world, while China is a well-tuned forward-looking focused powerhouse. The US military struggles in maintaining its strength because of cutbacks and sequestration, while China's military enjoys robust yearly increases in funding. The US military keeps retrofitting age-old weaponry while China keeps fielding all types of modern armaments. The US military has to beg for R&D funds for new weaponry and gets a pittance from Congress, while the China military can count on almost unlimited funds for advanced weaponry research and development. US politicians keep wasting trillions of dollars on misguided overseas operations and conflicts, while China keeps building up and modernizing its arsenal. The US keeps adhering to outdated Cold War treaties with Russia, while China is going all out unhindered in developing and deploying whatever weapons it wants. The US keeps living in the old US-Soviet Cold War mentality by misguidedly focusing on Russia, a country that's more of a regional power than a global one, while China keeps building up a superpower military that will challenge the US like no other power ever had. Chinese leaders have given free rein to the PLA in becoming more aggressive and expanding its power around the world, while US politicians keep gelding the US military: Obama, while grandiosely proclaiming the US pivot toward Asia, crippled the US military into a paper-tiger that China treated with utter disrespect, and Trump's foreign policy is that of retrenchment and focus on internal affairs.

The US did have many opportunities in the past to clip China's wings and maybe control its rise as a pacifist power à la Japan, or even partition it. The US could've decisively intervened in the Chinese Civil War on the side of the Nationalists to rout the communists but didn't. The US could've forcefully intervened when China invaded and occupied Tibet, but didn't. The US could've made China pay a heavy price in the Korean War, just as it did with Japan in World War II, but didn't and suffered a great and shameful defeat at the hands of China's peasant army, which pushed the US Army back across the 38° parallel.

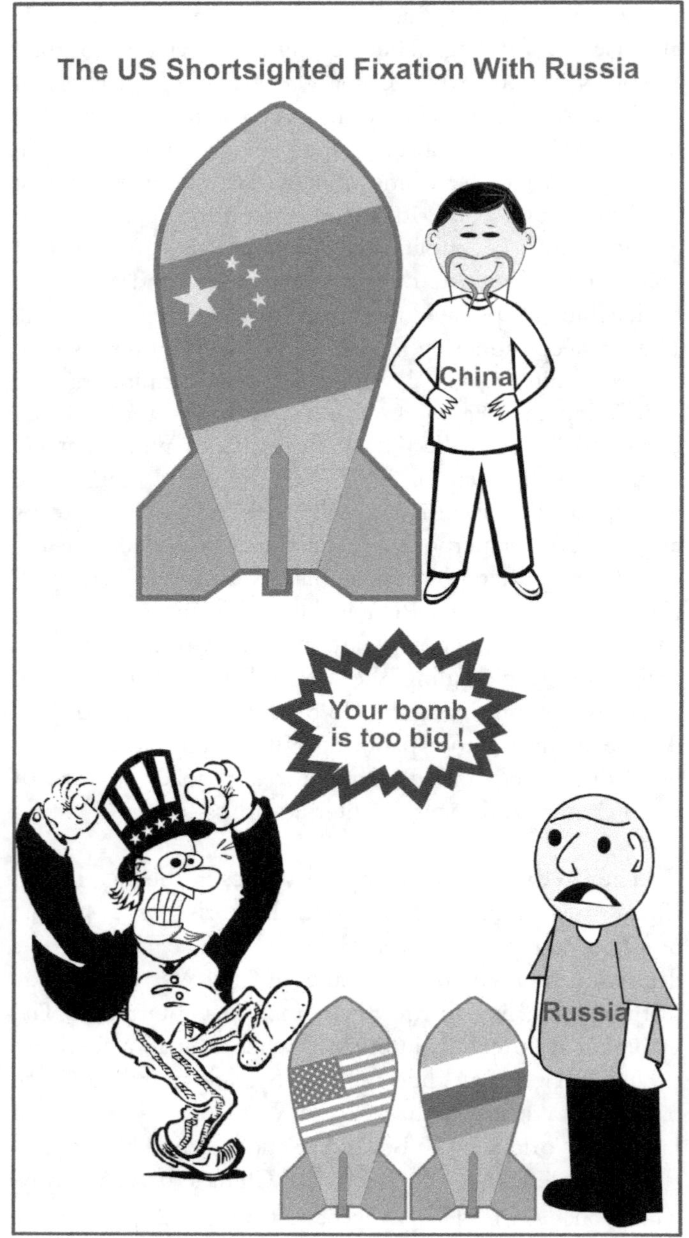

The US Shortsighted Fixation With Russia
China
Your bomb
is too big !
Russia

The US could've found a way to block communist China from becoming a member of the US Security Council, but didn't and instead embarked on a misguided and fawning engagement with China, starting with the Nixon administration. The US could've a long time ago supported Taiwan's outright independence, but again never dared to antagonize China. And the US could've stopped China from claiming all of the South China Sea and building artificial islands, but again chose the escapist way of calling for dialog while China kept building and fortifying its Paracel and Spratly Islands bases.

Now China has developed a strong enough military to intimidate US politicians and deter any US military moves against it. China has now assured that when it comes to the race for military supremacy, time is on its side, and any future conflict with the US will be on its own terms.

China now is in the driving seat on when and how the war with the US will break out. China knows that the US is mired in too many problems and is too hesitant to escalate tensions, and China knows how to take advantage of that. China knows how to push its agenda far enough and piece by piece without any significant US pushback. Thus, in the South China Sea, China is succeeding in its goal to control all of it by taking a gradual approach. Each time the US vociferously complains about one of its moves in the South China Sea, China takes a break from its activities to let things cool down a bit, and then pushes on again. Using such an approach, China has already built up important bases in the South China Sea, and will soon make them fully operational.

This gradual approach to military supremacy can be seen in the philosophy of former paramount leader Deng Xiaoping when he said, "Hide our strength, and bide our time." This stealth approach has suited China well in its rise. And now that China has achieved enough of a military deterrent, it's no longer shy about its intentions and has become quite aggressive this decade.

So how has China been preparing for war with the US? First, China has been aggressively boosting its military spending over the past three decades. According to GlobalSecurity.org, China's defense spending has increased by an average of almost 13% annually since 1989. And going forward, even as China's economy cools off, the Chinese military can still expect robust annual increases in its budget. Already, based on Purchasing-Power-Parity GDP, China's military budget is about 2/3 that of the US. And the gap between the two countries is closing fast.

It's expected that in about two decades, China's military budget will outright overtake that of the US. One thing that makes this reversal in standings inevitable is that whereas in China the military can count on the steadfast support of the CPC, in America the defense budget is subject to the machinations, whims, and vagaries of the ever-unpredictable US domestic politics.

China has been plowing huge sums of funding into its armed forces because, from the time of the former paramount leader Deng Xiaoping, Chinese leaders knew that the PLA's arsenal was terribly antiquated and that they needed to close the technology gap with the US military. Building a modern military was one pillar of Deng Xiaoping's Four Modernizations initiative. The PLA's modernization drive initially focused on building a strong national defense, and then once China grew stronger, it switched to offensive weaponry, such as aircraft carriers and stealth aircraft.

Second, in order to fast close the technology gap and catch up with the US military, China has pulled out all the

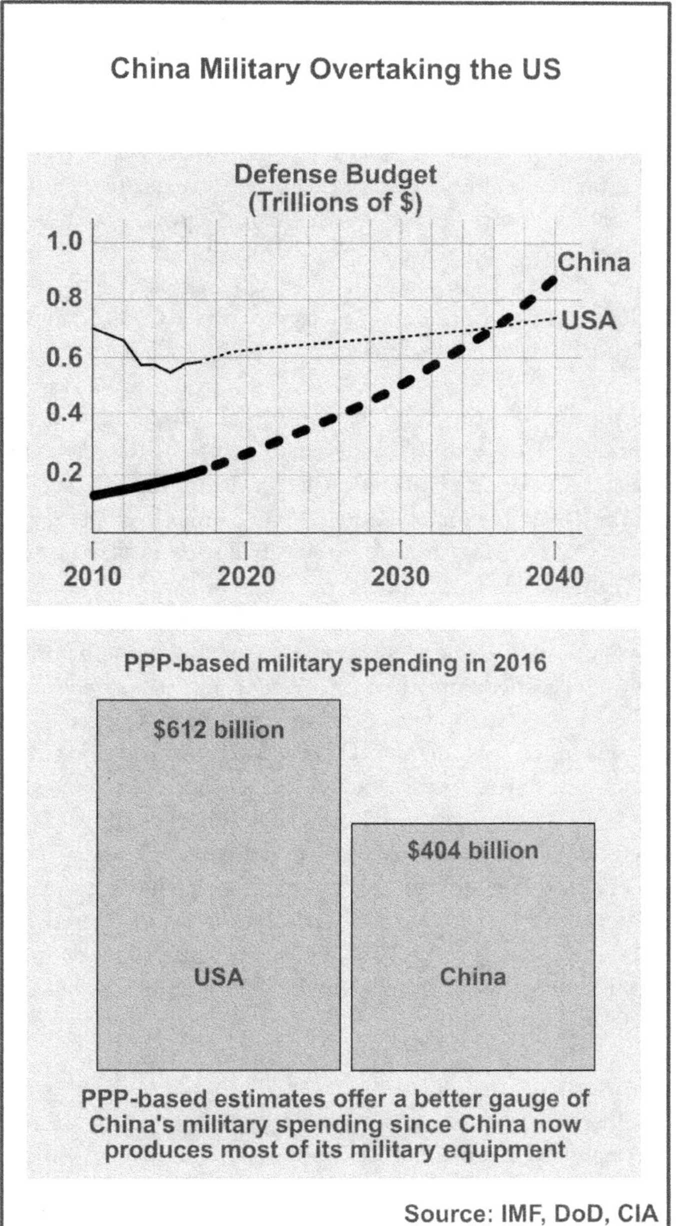

China Military Overtaking the US
Defense Budget
(Trillions of $)
1.0
0.8
0.6
0.4
0.2
China
USA
2010
2020
2030
2040
PPP-based military spending in 2016
$612 billion
$404 billion
USA
China
PPP-based estimates offer a better gauge of
China's military spending since China now
produces most of its military equipment
Source: IMF, DoD, CIA

stops and used every means necessary to acquire the necessary technology. This has meant hacking US defense companies and using spies to steal US defense secrets, reverse-engineering US and Russian weaponry, buying Western high-tech companies with portfolios that can help the Chinese military, and innovating. For example, a 1999 Congress report, known as the Cox Report, stated that China had stolen classified information on every thermonuclear warhead in the US arsenal, and that included intercontinental ballistic missiles, short-range ballistic missiles, and submarine-launched ballistic missiles.

Another example is that using industrial and cyber espionage, China stole the defense secrets of the US most advanced weapons like the F-35, the F-22, the B-2 stealth bomber, the advanced Patriot PAC-3 missile system, the Army's system for shooting down ballistic missiles known as Terminal High Altitude Area Defense or THAAD, the Navy's Littoral Combat Ship, space-based lasers, missile navigation and tracking systems, as well as a trove of other highly classified information. According to documents leaked by whistleblower Edward Snowden, Chinese F-35 espionage efforts in the US focused on acquiring the plane's electro-optical targeting system, engine and fuselage schematics, and radar-absorbing coatings. The documents estimate that many terabytes of data were stolen and used in the design of China's newest stealth fighters, the J-31 and J-20. The Chinese also targeted US allies and their companies. Thus, an Australian defense firm involved in developing the F-35 fighter jet was hacked in 2016.

Another example is that China has been using many Chinese Americans and Chinese nationals living in the US to steal US defense secrets. Thus, a naturalized Chinese American who worked at NASA on the space shuttle program gave highly sensitive information about military and space-related technology to Chinese handlers. Another naturalized Chinese American supplied China with information on US ships and submarines. Another Chinese-American woman conspired with her Chinese handlers to illegally send a missile-firing drone and jet fighter engines to China. A Chinese national hacked into the computer networks of major US defense contractors, and stole military plans for the F-35 and F-22 fighter jets, and the C-17 military transport aircraft. And Chinese nationals and Chinese Americans who worked on sensitive and top-secret military projects, such as nuclear weapons, in famous labs, such as the Los Alamos National Laboratory in New Mexico and the Lawrence Livermore National Laboratory in California, and for defense contractors, such as Boeing, have gone back to China where they are using their acquired knowledge, skills and learned secrets to help the Chinese military machine.

China's state-guided and unprecedentedly large-scale hacking and stealing of US military secrets has allowed it to narrow, and in some instances close, the technology gap with the US over a relatively short period of time. By hook or by crook, China has been able to build a strong defense industry that in some fields can match the US. For example, China is now developing leading-edge weapon systems such as quantum radars to detect stealth jets, quantum-communication satellites to resist hacking, and drones that can fight in swarms. Importantly, the PLA's modernization drive has allowed it to deploy a credible strategic nuclear deterrent against the US and others, and a national defense system that can keep enemy forces at bay far away from China's shores. This defense system has an A2/AD (Anti-Access, Area Denial) capability that can wreak havoc on US forces in case of a conflict in China's vicinity.

Third, China under the leadership of the present

paramount leader Xi Jinping realized that its armed forces, when compared to those of the US, were hampered by outdated Soviet-era command structures that severely crippled the PLA's ability to fight and win modern wars even though it was flush with funds and cutting-edge weaponry. Indeed, the PLA had been dominated by the army or ground force, and had become a bureaucratic, complacent, and corrupt behemoth with many entrenched interests, a situation which not only represented a danger to the country, but even more importantly a danger to the power of the CPC. Thus, Xi Jinping decided to institute a far-reaching organizational reform of the PLA, with the aim of making the PLA into a more effective and lethal military that is commensurate with the aspirations and lofty goals of the "China Dream."

The restructuring, slated to be completed by 2020, includes consolidating the military regions into battle zones or theater commands, instituting joint-commands, trimming non-essential personnel, weeding out corrupt senior officers, enhancing discipline and CPC loyalty, strengthening the different forces, especially the Navy, Air Force, and Rocket Force, and establishing a new force, the Strategic Support Force. The restructuring will result in a lean and effective military where the CMC and CMC chairman-cum-commander-in-chief are in complete control of the PLA, the different services are responsible for the building and administration of their forces, and the theater commands focus on combat readiness and war fighting.

With such a reform of the organization of its armed forces, China will be able to engage in modern warfare on many battlefields, just as the US does. For example, in case of a conflict in the South China Sea, the Southern Theater commander will be able to prosecute the conflict by bringing into play joint-force groups comprising Army,

Navy South Sea Fleet, Air Force, and Rocket Force units that are based in the Southern Theater Command. The commander can also count on the support of other theater commands.

Fourth, China recognizes the importance of securing its energy supplies, especially in the case of a war with the US. China remembers full well how the US and its allies embargoed Imperial Japan and cut off its oil supplies, forcing it to fight for survival by attacking Pearl Harbor.

China relies heavily on oil and gas imports, and is sucking up energy supplies from around the world, including the Middle East, Central Asia, Southeast Asia, Russia, Africa, Australia, and Latin America. China is the world's largest importer of oil, and imports now account for about 60% of its oil needs. China's appetite for energy seems insatiable and keeps growing.

And China recognizes the need to keep these imports flowing in case of a war with the US. Thus, China has struck deals with Russia and Central Asian countries to lay huge oil and gas pipelines to supply China. These land-based pipelines are relatively safe from a US attack.

In the case of the "Malacca Dilemma," a term coined by former Chinese paramount leader Hu Jintao to describe China's overreliance on the Malacca Strait for most of its oil imports, China has been building and planning alternatives to lessen its dependence on that strategic chokepoint, which could be blockaded by the US and its allies in case of a war with China. One alternative is the China-Myanmar Economic Corridor, which is already operational and pumps Middle East oil and Myanmar natural gas to southwest China. Another alternative that's been implemented is the China-Pakistan Economic Corridor, which will see the laying of a huge oil pipeline to

China Securing its Energy Supplies
China
Malacca Strait
1 Russia oil, and soon natural gas
2 Central Asia oil and natural gas
3 Middle East oil
4 North and Northeast Africa oil
5 Western and Southern Africa oil
6 China-Myanmar Economic Corridor (oil and gas)
7 China-Pakistan Economic Corridor
8 Kra Isthmus: possible canal to bypass Malacca Strait
China warships guarding its sea lines of communication

pump Middle East oil from the Gwadar port in Pakistan to western China. And another alternative to bypass the Malacca Strait is that China may build a canal across the Kra Isthmus in southern Thailand.

China also recognizes that in addition to building secure routes for its energy imports and storing oil in a national strategic oil reserve, it also needs its military to guard and defend its sea lines of communication. This need is one of the main reasons for China's "String of Pearls." Having the Chinese Navy patrolling the South China Sea and the Indian Ocean, and the Chinese Marines stationed in such strategic bases as Djibouti and Gwadar, gives China greater confidence in securing its energy supplies. Thus, in case the US tries to blockade the Malacca Strait, China's warships and submarines in the South China Sea and Indian Ocean will be expected to try to keep it open. In case, the US tries to blockade the Strait of Hormuz or Mandeb Strait, China will be in in a position to fight back with its warships and submarines in the Indian Ocean, and its marines based in Djibouti and Gwadar.

Fifth, China knows that just as securing energy resources is vitally important, so is securing mineral resources, especially those that fuel modern high-tech industries. With such a goal in mind, China has locked up mineral resources around the world and ensured a dominant control over critical materials such as rare earth minerals, gallium, graphite, lithium, indium, vanadium and cobalt. These minerals are vital to electric vehicles, solar panels, batteries, smartphones, wind turbines, satellites, lasers, jet engines, missiles, superconductors and semiconductors.

China achieved its goal by acquiring mines around the world, accumulating equities in foreign mining companies,

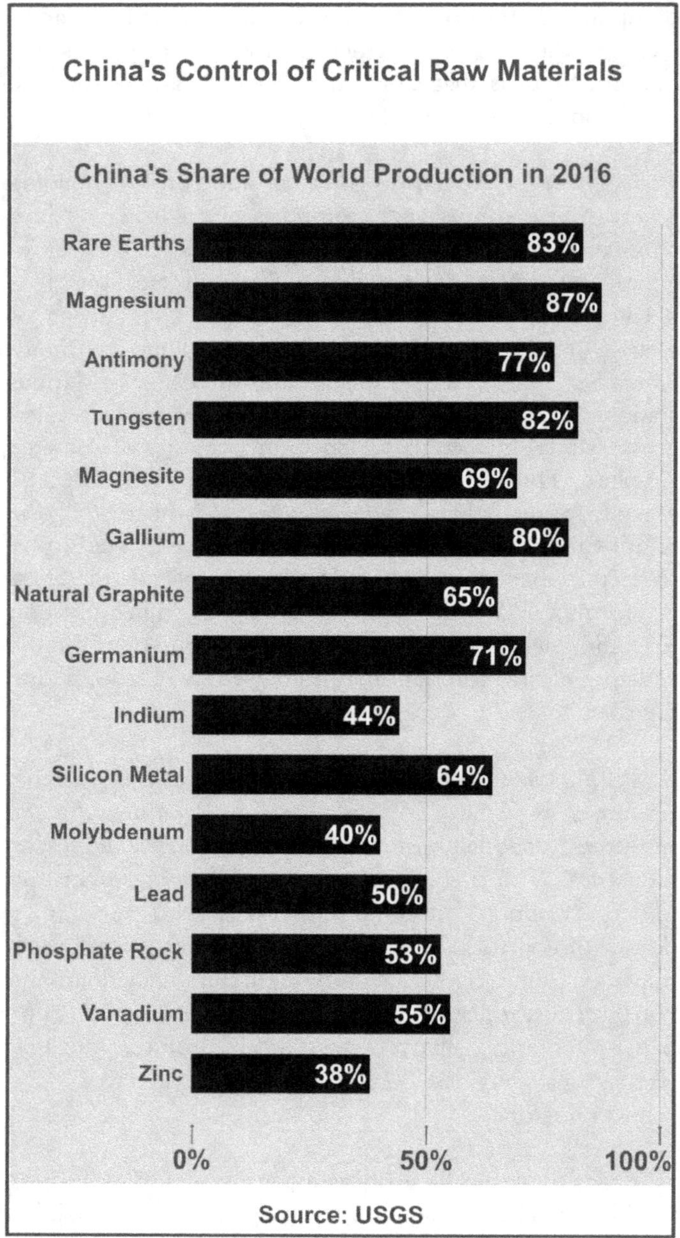

China's Control of Critical Raw Materials
China's Share of World Production in 2016
Rare Earths 83%
Magnesium 87%
Antimony 77%
Tungsten 82%
Magnesite 69%
Gallium 80%
Natural Graphite 65%
Germanium 71%
Indium 44%
Silicon Metal 64%
Molybdenum 40%
Lead 50%
Phosphate Rock 53%
Vanadium 55%
Zinc 38%
0%
50%
100%
Source: USGS

and signing long-term contracts to buy foreign mining companies' production. China used both its state-owned enterprises and private companies that it controlled to achieve its strategy in important places around the world, such as in the Democratic Republic of the Congo (DRC), which is home to half of the world's cobalt reserves, South Africa, which is home to 90% of the world's platinum reserves, Brazil, which is home to 80% of the world's niobium reserves, and Chile, which is home to 57% of the world's lithium reserves.

In the case of rare earths, China controls about 80% of their mining, refining and processing, and accounts for more than 80% of the US total imports of them. The US is in a precarious position and would face a crisis if China were to suddenly stop rare earths exports because it would take years, even decades, for the US to establish a viable domestic rare earths industry. If China were to carry out such a halt to exports, not only would the US civilian economy be severely affected but so too would be the military. As an example, according to a report by CBS's 60 Minutes program, a US F-35 fighter jet uses more than half a ton of rare earths.

Sixth, China has successfully waged a soft war to lull the US into complacency while cunningly disguising its aggressive militarist rise, all while acquiring as much knowledge from the US military as possible. Thus, China has taken advantage of America's openness, transparency, naiveté, and engagement to glean more secrets of the US military's ways and means, and to strengthen its hand in any future conflict.

One way that China has been able to gain more insight into the US military has been through exchanges between the militaries of the two countries. Such exchanges have in recent years become quite frequent, and these exchanges

US Critical-Minerals Imports from China

Minerals	Imports from China (2014-2017)	Applications
Rare Earths	80 %	Electronics, Batteries, Missiles, Jet engines
Bismuth	80 %	Ballistics, Radiation shield
Yttrium	76 %	Jet engines, Radar, Laser
Barite	63 %	Radiation shield
Antimony	58 %	Batteries
Germanium	58 %	Fiber optics
Graphite	37 %	Batteries, Fuel cells
Gallium	32 %	IC circuits, LEDs
Tungsten	32 %	Projectiles, Missiles
Indium	27 %	LCD screens
Tellurium	27 %	Solar cells

Source: USGS

are far more valuable and beneficial to China than to the US. Many naïve American leaders and military top brass think that such exchanges allow both sides to learn about each other, but they forget that China has more to learn from the US than the other way around. After all, in many of these exchanges, the US is like the teacher and China the student. These exchanges have become so skewed that PLA officers can crash US military conferences without even bothering to hide who they are.

And the US has been so asinine as to invite the Chinese navy to join military exercises near Hawaii. One can only guess how much the Chinese military relish such opportunities to practice for maybe a future visit to Hawaii, one not under such auspicious circumstances. The Chinese navy has also learned a lot about the US Navy when conducting anti-piracy operations in conjunction with the US. And the Chinese keep learning a lot more by being close to the US military. Thus, now that their Djibouti military base opened just miles away from that of the US, the Chinese will learn invaluable lessons on how to operate overseas by observing and keeping tabs on US forces.

The other way that China has been able to learn more about the US military, and the US as a whole, is through espionage. China is interested in information not only about the US military, but also about US companies, US organizations, and ordinary Americans.

Thus, the Chinese military infiltrated the Federal Deposit Insurance Corporation for many years and gained access to the banking records of millions of Americans. The Chinese also hacked many insurance companies, like Anthem, and hospitals and stole information on tens of millions of Americans. And in 2015, China hit the mother lode when it hacked the US Office of Personnel

China Cyber-espionage Attacks On the US

Each dot on the map represents
a Chinese cyber-espionage attack
on a corporate, private, or US Government victim.

Over the first five years of this decade,
China's intrusions numbered more than
600

The Northeast corridor from
Washington, D.C. to Boston
was blanketed with attacks

In California,
Silicon Valley
and the LA area
were heavily hit

Source: NSA, NBC

Management (OPM). According to the FBI, more than 20 million records were stolen in that hack. The information that was stolen by China is priceless and critically hurts the security of the US. That information includes names of personnel, dates of birth, social security numbers, addresses, and even more damaging security-clearance information, information that could be used to blackmail Americans for highly sensitive information.

In fact, no US entity is immune from China's espionage. A former NSA director said that China had hacked almost all major US companies, and in 2018 the FBI Director, Christopher Wray, said that China had been conducting espionage in all fifty US states.

And China is quite resourceful in finding effective and cunning ways of spying. For example, China uses women spies to extract information from US military and civilian personnel. In one instance, a Chinese female spy was able to get highly sensitive information from a defense contractor by dating him. The information included secret US war plans, nuclear weapons and deployment information, secrets on the MQ-9 Reaper drone, and a classified report titled "The Department of Defense China Strategy."

Another example of the Chinese cunning ways is that they bought or tried to buy property such as hotels and farms with militarily strategic values such as being close to army bases. In one instance, a Chinese government-controlled insurance company tried to buy a hotel for supposedly purely commercial purposes, but fortunately the deal fell through after US national security officials noted that it was located close to a US naval base.

China has also enlisted the help of its companies in its espionage efforts. For example, China Telecom Americas,

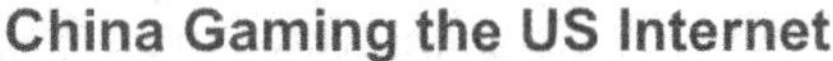

China Gaming the US Internet

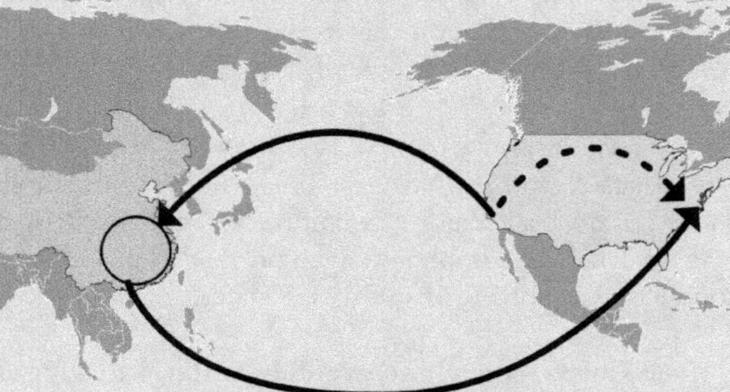

China Hijacking Internet Traffic
US domestic Internet traffic,
such as between LA and Washington, DC,
that should be routed inside the US,
is sometimes diverted through China
by China Telecom for nefarious purposes

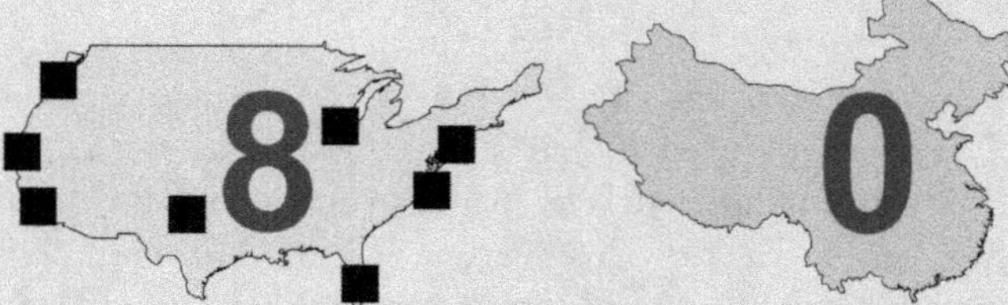

China's Access to the US Internet
.8
0
POPs in the US
owned by
China Telecom
POPs in China
owned by
US telecoms
Note: a POP is a network node/data center
Source: Ars Technica, PCMag, China Telecom Americas

which has a network covering the whole of the Continental US, diverted US Internet traffic through China on multiple occasions, giving China the opportunity to store and analyze that traffic.

Another example is that according to the US government, the Chinese telecom companies Huawei and ZTE export compromised equipment that allows China to conduct remote spying on the unsuspecting users. The equipment contains embedded software and hardware that can be used by China for nefarious purposes, such as surveillance and counterintelligence. The equipment could potentially even be remotely sabotaged and rendered inoperative in case of a conflict.

As further evidence, in 2018, Bloomberg reported that Chinese spies embedded tiny chips the size of rice grains into servers that made their way into the data centers of major US companies such as Amazon. The hack also affected the data centers of the US Department of Defense and the drone operations of the CIA. According to the report, the Chinese embedded the tiny microchips on the server motherboards manufactured in China. A security expert added that he had seen such hacks on a variety of hardware that was produced under contract in China.

In addition to helping China gain more insight into the US military and exploit its weaknesses, China's soft war has given it valuable time to enhance its position around the word and tilt the global battlefield in its favor in any future conflict with the US. China's extraordinary economic rise has given it ample resources to fund its military forces and buy influence around the world. China is no longer the insular kingdom of yore. China has become the world's economic engine and has built close relationships all around the world, relationships that come in handy during conflicts. China has already stamped its presence on its near seas and on the Indian Ocean with its "String of Pearls," and will undoubtedly keep extending this network of logistical support and influence around the world.

The valuable time that China gained by playing the US has already had a significant effect, which is that China has emerged as the dominant regional power and the US is no longer the undisputed power in the Western Pacific. The PLA's present strength gives the US pause before challenging China while the latter keeps bullying its neighbors, increasing its hegemony over East Asia, and extending its global reach.

Seventh, China has been preparing to sow chaos and discord inside the US in case a conflict breaks out between the two countries. China has heavily infiltrated many segments of the American society, especially the Chinese-American community, and many critical sectors of the economy. If China were to launch this "Hidden-Dragon" operation, its agents and moles could wreak havoc on the US financial markets, banks, electric grid, water supply, gas supply, transportation, Internet, and other sectors.

In 2014, the head of the NSA, Admiral Michael Rogers, told a congressional panel that China had the capacity to shut down the nation's power grid and other critical infrastructure through cyber attacks. The 2019 Worldwide Threat Assessment of the US Intelligence Community report reiterated that "China has the ability to launch cyber attacks that cause localized, temporary disruptive effects on critical infrastructure – such as disruption of a natural gas pipeline for days to weeks – in the United States." Such threats to the US critical infrastructure are real and waiting to go into effect. According to current and former national-security officials, the Chinese have penetrated many US utilities and implanted disruptive software programs that they could activate at any time.

Eighth, the PLA has laid out war plans and has been practicing how to fight and win against the US in the most likely location of a decisive Sino-US war: the Western Pacific. Such a conflict favors China since it's in its backyard. The PLA's goal is to inflict heavy losses on the US and emerge as the undisputed power in this part of the world. The PLA has drawn up plans for all eventualities, even for using preemptive strikes on the US forces as part of an active defense strategy.

In such a conflict, the US will rely on its air power from forward bases in the Western Pacific and naval power from its carrier strike groups. China knows that it has to go after those US forward bases in the first and second island chains, especially those in Japan and Guam, and also after the US carrier strike groups.

In the case of the US forward bases, China has been practicing how to completely destroy them or at least render them inoperable. According to a report on the website War on the Rocks, some satellite imagery of China's missile testing grounds shows China practicing bombing raids on what seems to resemble the Navy headquarters of the US Seventh Fleet in Japan. China has built up and deployed a formidable arsenal of powerful missiles for such a conflict. China will use concentrated attacks of ballistic missiles, and land, sea and air-launched cruise missiles to pummel US bases. China has improved the precision of its missile strikes through the deployment of ISR (Intelligence, Surveillance, Reconnaissance) capabilities such as over-the-horizon radar, satellites, manned aircraft, and long-endurance drones. China will also use its bombers, which have been practicing regular war maneuvers in the Western Pacific.

To counter US air power, China's fourth-generation and fifth-generation stealth aircraft can go head to head against US combat aircraft by using their improved avionics and longer-range air-to-air missiles, or they can engage in asymmetric fighting by going after US air-support aircraft such as the AWACS and tankers from safe distances. For US aircraft that manage to get close to China's shores, the PLA's SAM batteries, both indigenous and Russian-made, along China's coastline will rain missiles on those US aircraft. For instance, the S-400 air defense system that China bought from Russia can detect and shoot down targets including ballistic missiles, enemy jets and drones up to 373 miles away, at altitudes of between 33 feet and 17 miles.

As for the US carrier strike groups, the PLA Navy will counter by relying on its superiority in the number of warships, the longer-range of its missiles, and support systems such as undersea surveillance systems. China has been honing its tactics to deal heavy blows to the US Navy. Thus, Chinese warships have been shadowing US ships and even practicing mock attacks by engaging missile lock on them. According to a report by the Taiwanese paper Want China Times, the PLA is reported to have "sunk" a US aircraft carrier in a war game in the Gobi desert using its carrier-killer ballistic missile, the DF-21D, which has a range of about 1,250 miles, can reach a top speed of Mach 10, and is designed to destroy a US aircraft carrier in one hit. And in 2019, China launched its most powerful carrier-carrier ballistic missile, the DF-26, from Inner Mongolia to hit a target thousands of miles away in the South China Sea. China has stationed these missiles so far inland to keep them from being shot down by US interceptor missiles during the launch's vulnerable initial phase, the boost phase, during which the missile is climbing and gaining speed. The US carrier strike groups would have to try to shoot down these missiles during the terminal phase, an almost impossible task since during this phase the missiles are traveling so fast that the chance of their interception is very low.

And China knows that it has to go after the US command and control infrastructure, especially its eyes in the sky. Thus, China has practiced attacks against US satellites by test-firing lasers at them, test-firing anti-satellite missiles that reach near geosynchronous heights, and also by shooting down one of its own satellites.

The CPC will under no circumstance accept a defeat, for such acceptance would lead to its downfall from power and the possible breakup of China. If China's conventional forces come up short and face defeat, the CPC will go all out and resort to nuclear weapons even though China claims that it will not be the first to use nuclear weapons in a conflict. The Chinese don't have the West's qualms and considerations for minimizing collateral damage and civilian casualties. Just as China has thrown millions of its hordes in past wars, it will have no compunction about nuking millions of foreigners.

China has enhanced the survivability of its nuclear ballistic missiles against a US or other enemy's nuclear strike by making them mobile, such as on submarines or by hiding them underground in a system of hardened tunnels that stretch for thousands of miles, a system that's referred to as the Underground Great Wall of China. China has also been upgrading its ICBMs with MIRVs (Multiple Independently-targetable Re-entry Vehicles). These multiple nuclear warheads can overwhelm the US anti-missile defenses, not just because of their huge number, but also because of their maneuverability and the use of decoys and jammers.

China's arsenal of nuclear ballistic missiles is quite ominous. The DF-5 ICBM comes equipped with a nuclear warhead, and has a range long enough to easily hit targets throughout the US. The DF-31AG mobile ICBM can be armed with multiple nuclear warheads, can be mounted on all-terrain vehicles, and can hit targets throughout the US mainland. The DF-41, China's latest ICBM, is road-mobile, has the longest range of any nuclear missile in the world, and can carry up to a dozen nuclear warheads. The DF-26 intermediate-range ballistic missile can be armed with nuclear warheads and has a range of roughly 2,500 miles. It's been nicknamed the *Guam Killer* because it can hit that island from bases anywhere in China. The DF-17 hypersonic ballistic missile is capable of traveling at ten times the speed of sound. It's designed to fly fast and low so as to avoid detection and hit a target before any countermeasures can be taken. The missile has a range of about 1,500 miles and can carry a nuclear payload. And the JL-2A submarine-launched ballistic missile is armed with a nuclear warhead. According to the US DoD, it has a range of about 4,500 miles, and China currently deploys four Jin-class nuclear ballistic missile submarines each armed with 12 of these missiles. The JL-2A will soon be replaced by the more powerful JL-3, which will carry 10 MIRVs, each containing multiple nuclear warheads.

The uncomfortable truth is that China's strategy of taking on the US military has succeeded. China is no longer afraid of aggressively defending its interests even when antagonizing the US.

While China is still far from its goal of global military supremacy, it has already mostly achieved the first phase of that goal, the phase of being the dominant regional power in the Western Pacific. China is now actively pushing ahead with its agenda of hegemony over East Asia, aggressively asserting and consolidating its claims in its

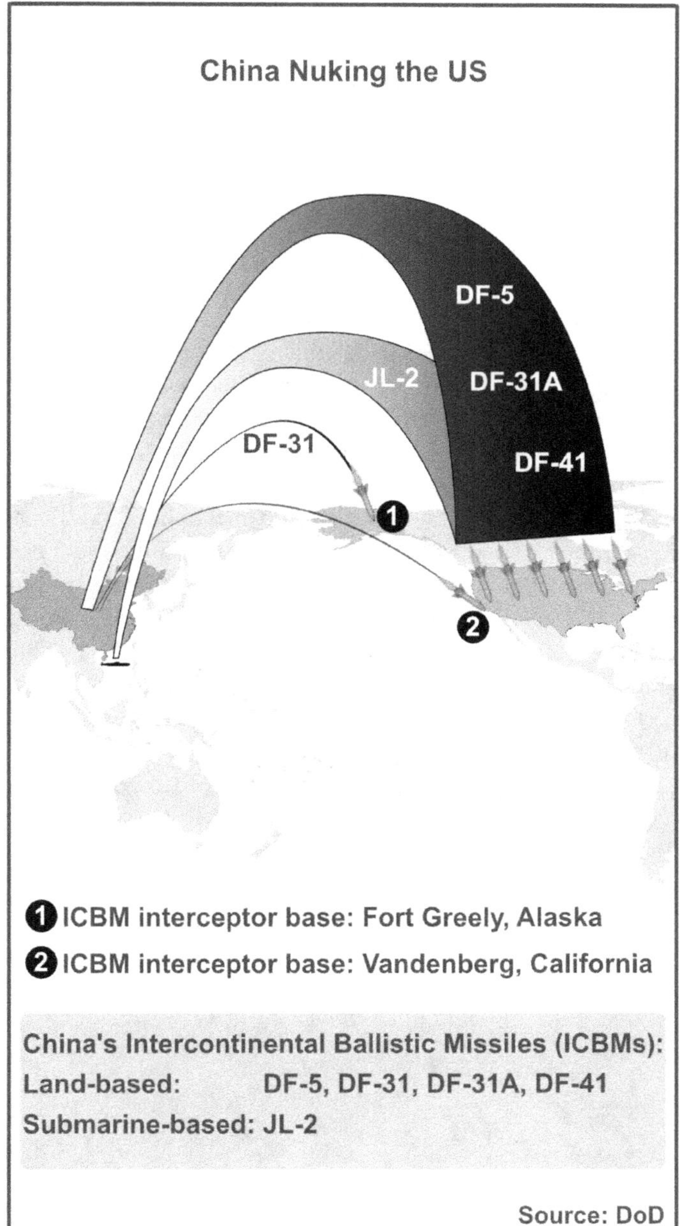
China Nuking the US
DF-5
JL-2
DF-31A
DF-31
DF-41
1
2
1 ICBM interceptor base: Fort Greely, Alaska
2 ICBM interceptor base: Vandenberg, California
China's Intercontinental Ballistic Missiles (ICBMs):
Land-based: DF-5, DF-31, DF-31A, DF-41
Submarine-based: JL-2
Source: DoD

near seas, and growing its might in the Indian Ocean.

And China is working hard on leapfrogging the US in future warfare, such as with quantum communications, quantum radar, and drone warfare. For example, China is developing ghost-imaging satellites that use quantum physics to detect US stealth planes like the B-1 bomber. These satellites can see through darkness and clouds.

China has executed its strategy to perfection. It's rising to be a mighty power that's unlike anything the US has ever faced. China will dwarf the Nazi Germany and Imperial Japan that the US faced in World War II, and China will not be the hobbled Soviet Union that the US faced in the Cold War. China is an entirely different kind of beast. Not only is it an economic and military colossus, but it's also a solid homogenous block of mainly one racial group, the Han, who outnumber any other ethnic group in the world and who survived together for millennia while other groups disintegrated and faded into history. This mass of people is now more unified than ever under the CPC and marching to its orders. China is already a formidable power, and the scary thing is that it's still in the early stages of its rise. In about a couple of decades, China will be the most powerful nation in the world and the center of global power, a tribute to its old moniker of Middle Kingdom.

For the rising and domineering China, the world preeminence awaits. For the US and the West, the long slide to oblivion and Han hell has already begun.

7

EPILOG

If things keep going the way they have, China will without a shred of a doubt become the dominant global superpower, eclipsing the US and all other countries in the economic, scientific, military, and political fields. The facts and numbers are just undeniable. China has the huge number of people that no other power has. China has the homogeneity of people and focus of government that no other power has. China has the largest mass of educated people in the world. China has the determination and discipline that no other power has. China has the biggest economy in the world by some estimates, and soon will be the biggest by all estimates. China has built up a formidable military that soon will be second to none. And China has two big motivations to realize its goal of world supremacy: one is to regain its status of centuries past as the word's center of power, and another is to exact revenge on the West and other powers for its century of humiliation.

Not only is China fast charging to global supremacy, but it's also marginalizing the West and other powers in the process, and reshaping the world in its image, an image of trampling on the Western ideals of democracy, human rights, civilized behavior, and living in harmony with nature. China is stamping its hegemony over its neighbors and domination over the world, and like a chain of dominoes, the world's countries have been falling one by one under China's influence and control.

China's confidence and aggressiveness look unstoppable. It's on its way to world preeminence in all spheres and to realizing the "China Dream," a dream that unfortunately is a nightmare for many, especially the West.

For the West, continuing on the path of engaging with or containing China has proven to be ineffective and has not succeeded in reigning China or getting it to behave as a responsible power. China only understands force. However, Western leaders lack the fortitude to stand up to China. Their indecisiveness and lameness borders on stupidity and cowardice, and only adds to China's transgressions and menace.

What can the West do? First of all, only the US may be able to do something about China. Europe, well, it's truly the old and tired continent. It's hopelessly divided and lazily going through a slow decline to irrelevance. As for the US, American leaders have continuously proven to be overly cautious and either weak or naïve with regards to China. Sometimes it seems that the shock drubbing at the hands of China's peasant army in the Korean War still haunts American souls. It's very unlikely that the US will ever risk going to war against China, except in the case of a Chinese attack on American soil or military. The fact is that the US has grown inherently weak at the core, and its leaders don't have the grit to really take on China.

Here's an example of the sorry state of the US response to China's menace. In the South China Sea, China built up

Weak US

Obama Bowing to Chinese Communists

Obama bowed in a markedly sickening way to
Chinese strongmen Hu and Xi
when greeting them

Obama Insulted by Philippines President

When Duterte,
a real moron, a retard,
the president of a banana republic,
a Third World country, an insignificant country,
a weaker-than-weak county,
a former US colony,
a country dependent on the US for its defense,
a shithole by Trump's definition, ...
when this real ape dares to publicly call Obama,
the president of the United States,
"a son of a whore,"
then nothing more needs to be said
about the sorry state that the US has descended to

reefs into artificial islands and fortified them as military bases with runways for its combat jets, ports for its warships, radar systems, and many types of missiles. And after all that, in 2016, in a hearing before the US Senate Armed Services Committee, the admiral in charge of the US Pacific Command stated, "In my opinion, China is clearly militarizing the South China Sea." In his opinion? This is akin to a man walking in on his wife in bed having wild sex with another man, and then saying to himself, "I believe my wife is cheating on me!" Duh, you think? This is the state of American affairs where even those fully aware of China's grave transgressions are afraid to describe those transgressions in clear absolute terms, and have to mollify and sugarcoat their statements in subjective terms.

Another example is that of former vice-president and 2020 presidential contender Biden. This guy, a carbon copy of the weakling Obama, said in 2019, "China is going to eat our lunch? Come on, man! They're not bad folks, folks." This perfectly illustrates the ignorance and weakness of US political leaders that have allowed China to become the existential threat that it is.

The fact is that the US has never dared to take on the PLA directly. In China's Civil War, instead of supporting its ally, the KMT, and crushing the communists, the US played the role of mediator and the Chinese communists won. In the Korean War, the US lost thousands of troops and was pushed back by the Chinese communists, and instead of bombing the Chinese to submission like it did with Japan, the US accepted its heavy casualties and a divided Korea. In Tibet, when the Chinese communists invaded, the US didn't intervene or do much to help the Tibetan resistance. In the Vietnam War, the Chinese communists supported North Vietnam inflict heavy casualties on the US, and yet the US didn't dare confront China. And nowadays, in the South China Sea, while China

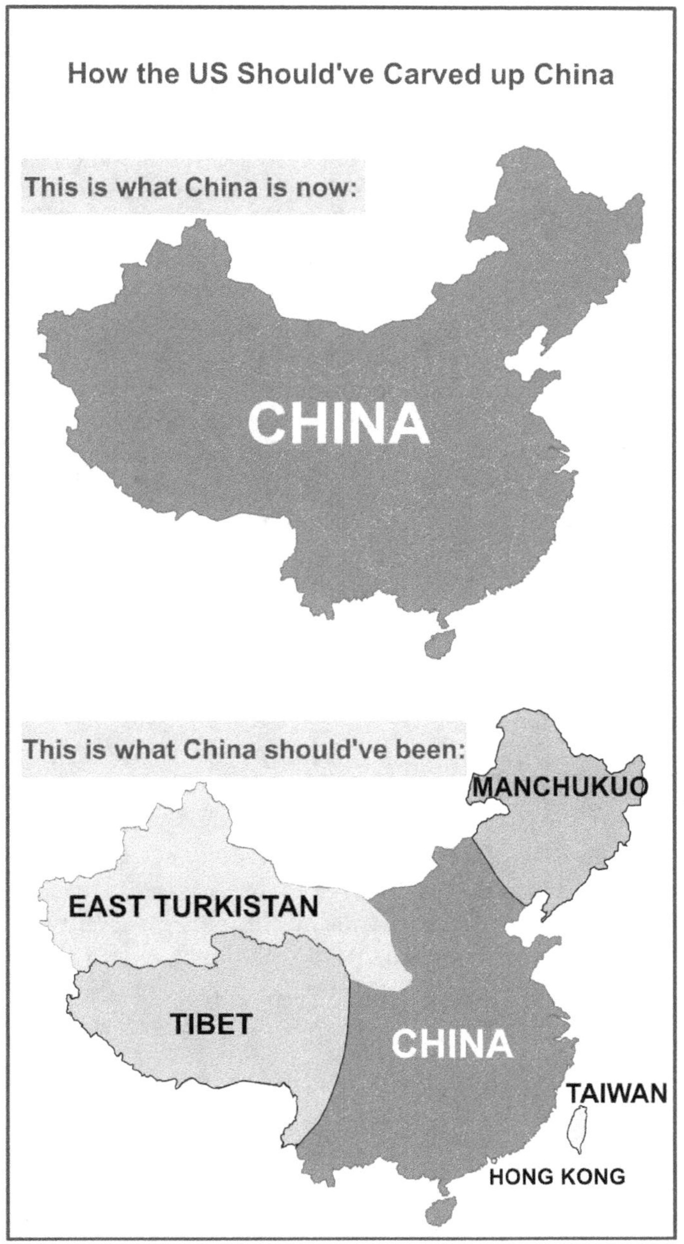

How the US Should've Carved up China

This is what China is now:

CHINA

This is what China should've been:

MANCHUKUO

EAST TURKISTAN

TIBET

CHINA

TAIWAN

HONG KONG

keeps building and fortifying its illegal military installations, the US doesn't dare to directly challenge China like former Secretary of State Tillerson suggested when he stated that the US should not only stop China building those islands, but also should deny China access to them. Instead, the US keeps nudging ASEAN nations to confront China. Such shirking of responsibility and hiding behind others borders on cowardice. Even the Philippine president Duterte, a guy not known for his intellect, saw though the US cowardice and called the US out for its pussyfooting. He said that the US keeps urging the Philippines to get tough on China in the South China Sea dispute and to confront the PLA's establishing of artificial bases. He rightly added that if the US was so incensed about China's expansionism, then why didn't the US directly confront China. After all, the US keeps saying that those artificial islands are illegal. However, true to form, the US just keeps complaining while China keeps building and fortifying. To China and others, the US seems like a barking dog that the Chinese keep ignoring. All the US dares to do is conduct harmlessly laughable so-called freedom of navigation patrols miles away from those islands.

So, can China be forced to mend its wayward ways? In the economy, can China be made to play by the rules like everyone else? In environmental protection, can China's raping of our planet be brought to an end? In politics, can China's export of authoritarianism and disregard for human rights be stopped? And in the military, can China be contained? The answers to these questions leave no doubt as to the great menace that China represents for the US and the rest of the world.

In the economy, China steals, China lies, China breaks its promises, and China doesn't abide by international rules. In trading with the US and the rest of the world, China has gotten away with murder. Lame US political and business leaders have stood by and greedy Wall Street has cheered while China kept raping America for decades, wrecked its manufacturing, and drained its wealth.

America's, and actually the world's, only hope of confronting China and forcing it to play by the rules could only come from an American nationalist leader, a non-politician, one who's not beholden to special interests. That has happened with the election of Trump, who for all his flaws and deficiencies of character has at least had the courage to forcefully confront China. It remains to be seen whether he'll succeed as he has already shown that he and his family could be manipulated by China and Wall Street. China will in most likelihood just appease him with some promises that it will break later on when he leaves office.

The fact is that the US not only doesn't have the fortitude to confront China, but neither does it have the leverage it used to. US sanctions, tariffs and other maneuvers will not make China beg for mercy. China has become self-sufficient in key technologies and become the leading trading partner of most countries. Economically, China is unstoppable not only because of its might and determination, but also because of the US's weakness and indecision.

China will not only continue to be the engine of the world economy, but it will also become the dominant world economy. And to China, being dominant means winning everything. It means having its currency as the global currency of choice. It means having new world financial institutions under its control. It means the Chinese holding all the strings and bossing everyone else around.

If the US were really determined to confront China about the economy, then first and foremost the US should not let China get away with its past infractions, those of committing the biggest heist of riches in history. China should not get to keep its ill-gotten riches without a penalty. The US cannot ignore China's rape of the US economy, and must make China pay for stealing trillions of US dollars from the US. The US should slap China and its enterprises, especially the likes of Alibaba and Huawei, with an "Original Sin" tax in the hundreds of billions of dollars, a tax that should be high enough to cancel the US debt to China.

And going forward, the US must force China to stop its illegal practices of stealing IP, coercing US companies to reveal trade secrets, unfair subsidies to its companies, anti-foreign-competition legislation, dumping, and corrupt dealings around the world. The US cannot just rely on agreements with China because the latter can never be trusted to honor its commitments. The US must put in place supervisory mechanisms to keep China under a constant watch, and implement immediate and severe penalties for any Chinese infractions.

In the environment, China is ravaging our planet and gobbling up its resources at unsustainable rates that the world has never seen before, China is threatening and wiping out the world's wildlife like no other country ever had, and China is polluting our planet in apocalyptic ways that threaten our planet's climate and humanity's very existence.

China has continued its rape of our planet while ignoring the concern of the rest of the world, and would have continued doing so were it not for nature striking back. Indeed, China's breakneck industrialization has harmed its environment to such an extent that pollution has become a huge health problem in China, killing millions of people each year. China's air, water bodies and soil have become polluted and contaminated to such a large scale and alarming levels that China had no choice but to start paying attention to its ill-advised environment-wrecking habits and policies.

Another way that nature struck back to get China to pay heed to its uncivilized treatment of our planet was when it struck China with the deadly epidemic of SARS that killed thousands. However, nature needs the help of the rest of the world to get China to mend its wayward ways.

Unfortunately, the international treaties on protecting the environment and wildlife haven't been sufficient so far in containing China's menace to our planet. If the US were really determined to confront China about the protection of our planet, then the US must get tough on China and not let it shirk its responsibility to our planet through the lame claims of being a developing country. China is a monster that's wrecking our planet like no other country ever had before, and the US must make sure that China is held to the same tough standards as any developed country. The US should levy pollution tariffs on imports from China, and impose sanctions on any Chinese involved in harming protected wildlife.

In politics, China has been winning the ideology war with the US both domestically and on the world stage. Domestically, China has effectively insulated its populace from foreign media and brainwashed it into complete submission through an unrelenting jingoistic and xenophobic propaganda.

And on the world stage, China has expanded its influence because most of the countries in the world are far from being democracies and thus are receptive to China's system of authoritarianism. The sorry state of democracies in the US and Europe has also been a great factor in pushing the world toward such authoritarianism.

China actively supports dictatorships and oppressive governments around the world and shields them from sanctions from the West. Thus, when a country like Myanmar commits genocide against the Rohingyas, a genocide documented by the UN and rights groups, China has no qualms about defending such a despicable government at the United Nations Security Council.

If the US were really determined to confront China about its politics, then the US needs to confront China head on. The US must wake up to China's growing menace within its borders. In this regard, the US must require the Confucius Institutes and all Chinese media to register as foreign agents, and the US must restrict their operations in the US unless China agrees to reciprocity by providing US media with equal access to the China market. The US must also expel from the US any Chinese, whether a student, a scholar, a businessman, a visitor, a permanent resident or other, who in any way tries to stifle free speech or infringe on the rights of others.

The US has to take the fight to China's home turf and let the Chinese masses know about the systemic corruption, the lavish and decadent lifestyle of the governing elite and their rich cronies, the rampant abuse of human rights, the abject state of rural migrants, the mass surveillance, and the persecution of minorities. The US can't let China brainwash domestic and world audiences with the false image of China as a utopian country under the leadership of the CPC.

The US has to champion the causes of China's oppressed minorities, especially the Tibetans and Uighurs. The US must impose severe sanctions on officials and companies that support repression in Tibet and Xinjiang.

And on the world stage, the US has to fight China's nefarious and pernicious influence in countries around the world by exposing China for the repressive regime that it is. In countries that are in bed with China, the US must sanction the regimes of those countries, implement drastic trade restrictions on their economies, and work with the local opposition in such countries to wrestle them away from China's grip. Such local opposition is always present wherever the Chinese are. The US should have no qualms about toppling such regimes because they are without exception corrupt and authoritarian, and because the fate of democracy is at stake.

Finally, in the military, China has become a great power that's fast growing in might and reach. China is bullying its neighbors, challenging the US, and extending its influence around the world. Given the fast pace of its development and modernization, China will surely overtake the US as the dominant global military power if nothing is done to stop it.

If the US were really determined to confront China about its military ambitions, then what can the US do? The grim truth is that China's military might has reached such a dangerous stage of development that the only effective way of reining it is for the US to undertake the following drastic measures.

First and foremost, the US needs to come to its senses and realize that its greatest existential threat is China, not Russia. Russia is hampered by many factors that will always restrict it to being a major but regional power. And Russia, unlike China, isn't out to devour the world. Russia just wants respect from the West. And Russia shares many historical, religious and racial bonds with the West, bonds that are alien to China.

Second, the US must realize that it's already in a Cold War with China.

Third, the US has to realize that whereas it was able to win the previous Cold War by waiting out, outspending and bankrupting the Soviet Union, the US will not be able to do the same with China. If anything, China might be able to outspend and bankrupt the US.

Fourth, the US has to realize that war with China is inevitable. The US must understand that there will be no peaceful coexistence with China when the latter becomes the dominant power. China believes that its relationship with the US is a zero-sum game that it has to win.

Fifth, the US must realize that any military treaties with Russia unnecessarily hinder it while China keeps expanding its military. Thus, the US must develop all kinds of short and medium-range missiles and deploy them in Asia, on the doorsteps of China.

Sixth, the US must realize that in a conflict with China, the US must be ruthless like never before in its history. With the Chinese, you have to shoot first and ask questions later. If you engage or reason with them, you lose. If you trust them, you lose. In fact, the crazy thing is that if you treat them as your equals, you lose. The only way to get to them is with force - brutal, lethal and uncompromising force.

Seventh, the US has to realize that the sooner the war happens, the better for it as it still has a military advantage, one that incidentally is fast disappearing. The window for containing and neutering China is almost gone, and action is needed immediately because China is fast developing

How the US Can Stop the China Menace

 **Economy:**

- ❖ *Cancel US debt to China for its past infractions*
- ❖ *Force China to play by international rules*
- ❖ *Keep constant checks on China's acts*
- ❖ *Promptly and severely punish any infraction*

2 **Environment:**

- ❖ *Hold China to Western environmental standards*
- ❖ *Levy pollution tariffs on imports from China*
- ❖ *Sanction China for wildlife infractions*

3 **Politics:**

- ❖ *Take the ideology fight to China's turf*
- ❖ *Expose the CPC corruption and decadence*
- ❖ *List China's media in the US as foreign agents*
- ❖ *Counter China's global propaganda*
- ❖ *Sanction regimes that are allied with China*

 **Military:**

- ❖ *Clip the PLA's wings now before it's too late*
- ❖ *Stop China from fielding a blue-water navy*
- ❖ *Take out China's bases outside the mainland*
- ❖ *Take out any Chinese assets that venture out beyond the first island chain*
- ❖ *Station troops in Taiwan*
- ❖ *Actively work for the breakup of China*

into a power that the US wouldn't dare to challenge. If the US doesn't take any action, then by 2020, China will be undefeatable in its vicinity; by 2030, China will be the undisputed power in the Western Pacific and Indian Ocean; and by 2050, China will achieve world preeminence and dominance in every aspect.

The time to stop China is fast running out, and the US must stop militarily tiptoeing around China's bullying and expansionism. The way for the US to stop and contain China militarily now and forever is by restricting its military operating sphere to its mainland borders. This means restricting the PLA's maritime and air zones of operation.

In the maritime field, the US must put an end to China's blue-water navy. Thus, the US must blockade all the chokepoints in the first island chain and never let any Chinese naval vessel go past. China's warships, including its two aircraft carriers, must be restricted to China's ports and its mainland's territorial seas, meaning just a few miles from shore. The US Navy with its qualitative superiority can take out any Chinese naval vessels that try to venture out beyond this area. The US also needs to close China's bases in the South China Sea and Djibouti and deny China the ability to establish any bases anywhere in the world.

In the air, the US needs to set up a no-fly zone over the East China Sea and South China Sea that specifically targets China's air power and interdicts it from flying anywhere beyond its coast.

And finally, the US must once and for all put China in its place by recognizing Taiwan's independence and stationing troops there, and by actively working for the breakup of China.

If the US were to take these steps, the Chinese will most likely go to war, and the US has to be ready to strike China like it never had before because the Chinese will be ruthless and reckless. The nuclear option will probably come into play because China is a wickedly criminal regime and its "No-First-Use" policy is actually "No, First Use." The US must have plans in place to deal with this doomsday scenario.

These drastic steps are the only sure way to stop the China menace. Otherwise, it's game over for the US and the West.

Realistically though, the weak and irresolute US and West will not do much to stop China from reaching its goal of world dominance in every aspect. The Chinese are harder-working, more disciplined, more united, more determined, more focused, more zealous, and more patriotic. The century of China, and Asia in general, is already a fact, and the West's decline relative to Asia is unstoppable. The Han hordes will keep bulldozing their way around the world and China will keep riding roughshod over the West and everybody else. The sad reality is that the age of the West is fleeting away, and China has ushered in the Asian century where the "China Dream" reigns supreme.

REFERENCES

US sources:
US International Trade Commission
US Trade Representative (USTR)
US Department of Commerce (DOC)
US Department of Defense (DoD)
US Department of Justice (DOJ)
US Department of Homeland Security (DHS)
US Census Bureau
US Department of Energy (DOE)
US Energy Information Administration (EIA)
Central Intelligence Agency (CIA)
National Security Agency (NSA)
Federal Bureau of Investigation (FBI)
National Counterintelligence and Security Center (NCSC)
National Science Foundation (NSF)
US Geological Survey (USGS)
US Embassy, Beijing, China
Congress Reports

World organizations sources:
International Monetary Fund (IMF)
The World Bank
United Nations Food and Agriculture Organization (FAO)
United Nations Office on Drugs and Crime (UNODC)
Organization for Economic Cooperation and Development (OECD)
World Health Organization
World Tourism Organization

International institutions sources:
European Environment Agency
AML RightSource
Global Financial Integrity
McKinsey Global Institute
Center for Strategic International Studies

Top500
Institute of International Education
Heritage Foundation / American Enterprise Institute.

China sources:
People's Bank of China
Chinese Ministry of Education
Chinese Ministry of Defense

Media sources:
Reuters
Bloomberg
BBC
CNBC
ABC
CBS
NBC
FOX News
The National Interest
The Diplomat
Time
NY Times
LA Times
Washington Post
The Guardian
South China Morning Post
The Economist
AppleInsider
BGR

Other sources:
The Travel Diaries of Albert Einstein: The Far East, Palestine, and Spain, 1922-1923, edited by Ze'ev Rosenkranz, Princeton University Press

www.ingramcontent.com/pod-product-compliance
Lightning Source LLC
Chambersburg PA
CBHW061752250726
48657CB00001B/83